Two Planks and A Passion

A Play

Anthony Minghella

Samuel French – London
New York – Sydney – Toronto – Hollywood

TWO PLANKS AND A PASSION

The play was first presented in 1983 at the Northcott Theatre, Exeter, in a production commissioned and directed by Stewart Trotter and designed by Tim Reed, with the following cast of characters:

Edward Young, Pinner's labourer	Keith Bartlett
Will Bluefront, Painter's labourer	David Oakley
Geoffrey Le Kolve, Master, Painter's Guild	
	Ted Valentine
Walter Paynter, apprentice painter	Sean Aita
Father Henry Melton, Pardoner and	
Chaplain to the Painter's Guild	Patrick Romer
Thomas Zachary, Painter's labourer	Mike Burnside
Sarah Zachary, his wife and lady-in-waiting	
to the Le Kolves	Heather Williams
Kathryn Le Kolve, wife of Geoffrey	Rosalind March
Richard II, King of England	Mark Jax
Robert de Vere, Earl of Oxford	Saul Reichlin
Anne of Bohemia, Queen of England	Amanda Orton
Alice Selby, Mayoress of York	Amanda Walker
William Selby, Mayor of York,	
Merchant	Raymond Cross
Jolyf Absolom, Herod in Merchants'	
play	David Oakley
Archbishop of York	Mike Burnside
God the Father	
Adam, a servant boy	

and assorted **gods, Christs, soldiers** and **crowd**

TWO PLANKS AND A PASSION

Subsequently the play was revised and presented at Greenwich Theatre in 1984 with the following cast of characters:

Edward Young, Pinner's labourer	David Fielder
Will Bluefront, Painter's labourer	Toby Salaman
Geoffrey Le Kolve, Master, Painter's Guild	
	Roger Sloman
Walter Paynter, apprentice painter	Chris Jury
Father Henry Melton, Pardoner and	
Chaplain to the Painter's Guild	Fred Pearson
Thomas Zachary, Painter's labourer	Chas Bryer
Sarah Zachary, his wife and lady-in-waiting	
to the Le Kolves	Corrine Ransome
Kathryn Le Kolve, wife of Geoffrey	Gillian Barge
Richard II, King of England	Michael Maloney
Robert de Vere, Earl of Oxford	Christopher Fulford
Anne of Bohemia, Queen of England	Cathryn Harrison
Alice Selby, Mayoress of York	Madge Hindle
William Selby, Mayor of York,	
Merchant	John Arthur
Jolyf Absolom, Herod in Merchants'	
play	David Fielder
Archbishop of York	Chas Bryer
God the Father	Toby Salaman
Adam, a servant boy	
and assorted **gods, Christs, soldiers** and **crowd**	

The play directed by Danny Boyle
Designed by Deirdre Clancy

This Acting Edition is based on the revised version of the play

ACT I

ACT II

The action of the play passes in and around the streets of York

Period: 1392

PRODUCTION NOTE

The setting for the play, when presented at Greenwich, was a large open stage with very little dressing. Two small raised areas, L and R break up the flatness of the area. The "common ground" on stage level represents several playing areas: outside the Pageant House; the Streets; the Mayor's garden; downstairs in the Selby household and Hen Street. The raised area SR represents the Mayor's bedroom. The raised area SL represents the dining-room in the Le Kolve house in Act I and Kathryn Le Kolve's bedroom in Act II.

Although the play is divided up into scenes this is merely to show where lighting changes and changes of mood occur. The action should flow smoothly and swiftly from one "scene" to the next, with no visible break.

Ideally, there should be an opening in the stage floor DSC into which the foot of the cross can be placed, for the rehearsal of the play.

ACT I*

SCENE 1

Bells for five. Late May. Early morning. 1392

Outside the Pageant House. This is a sort of medieval garage and is located in York. It houses the Pageant Wagon of the Painters' Guild, shared with the Pinners and Latterners. These three crafts play the Crucifixion Play, the thirty-fifth in the Corpus Christi Cycle

Will Bluefront and Edward Young appear, each dragging a plank of wood. During the scene they join the two planks into a cross by lashing the wood together with rope

Edward Don't it set your heart humming?

Will What?

Edward Doing this. Making the cross. Getting together. Saying the words.

Will Says my words every evening. Before I sleeps.

Edward Do you! And I do!

Will 'Stead of prayers.

Edward This is different though, eh? Every year I just have to see our wagon, have a dibble round the costumes, put on my helmet, pull out the planks and I gets a little flutter going.

Will (*grumpily*) I'm not starting before cakes and ale.

Edward Well, I doubt we'll get breakfast this year, Will. Everything's cut back, innit? I heard speak of another penny wanted from us for the play.

Will Who says? I'm not giving another penny. Anyway, we shouldn't have to pay if we're speaking in the pageant.

Edward That's all very well for our Guild, but say you were doing the *Harrowing of Hell*? Fifty odd nipper in that all told. If they never paid up there'd be no play.

Will That's the Merchants' do anyway. What's a penny to them? They shit pennies.

Edward I shit a shilling once. It hurt. Picked it up at a fair and swallowed it for safe keeping.

Will They gets ham at the Merchants' rehearsals. And best beer.

Edward Well . . . we gets the better play.

Will Now that's true. Where's the others then?

Edward Oh, be along shortly, I expect.

Will I half thought to find Thomas pinned up on the cross from last year.

---

*N.B. Paragraph 3 on page ii of this Acting Edition regarding photocopying and video-recording should be carefully read.

Edward Not like Walter to be late, mind.

Will He'll be sent to search for the priest who'll no doubt be sleeping somewhere he shouldn't.

Edward Shouldn't be rude about the parson, Will.

Will Well . . . If I puts my dick where I didn't ought it's a curse, Edward. If he do 'tis a blessing. Where's the fairness in that? So that's me and I'll not start before I'm given my breakfast.

Edward (*as a distraction*) Saw a dead heron this morning, me. That's bad luck. Means a famine.

Will Plague.

Edward Aye. Or plague.

Will No—just plague.

Edward Aye, it were a dead heron. Down by Ouse Bridge.

Will What do you do then? At night?

Edward What do you mean?

Will When you're doing your words . . . who does my part?

Edward Our missus. What about you?

Will No, I do it myself, me. I do all the parts.

Edward The whole play?

Will Aye.

Edward Oh.

Will I has to, Edward. I forget, see. Last year forgot my words, didn't I? Thought I'd get a fine.

Edward Not forgot. Stumbled.

Will Forgot.

Edward 'Tis easy done.

Will No. My brain's rusting. 'Nother year or two I'll be put out to pasture . . . I'll be off the wagon and down on the road pulling you boys round, station to station. Then you'll be first soldier.

Edward Well.

Will No, if I give him to anyone it'll be to you. Unless your missus do him very well! How is she?

Edward Oh, she's bonnie. Well, I say bonnie but you know she sold all her hair.

Will Never!

Edward Aye. Had a new babe see. Needed the money.

Will I never knew. What's that? Nipper?

Edward No. Little girl. Little lover, she is.

Will (*sympathetically*) Lovely red hair she had an' all, your missus.

Edward Aye.

Will Aye. If I pass him on to anyone will be to you, Edward.

Edward lifts up the cross

Edward Well, she's done then. Shall we have a go at it?

Will Aye.

Edward With the moves?

Will No, can't do the moves, can we, missing Thomas. No, just the parts.

Geoffrey Le Kolve and Walter approach

Geoffrey How do, lads?

Edward ⎫
⎬ (*together*) 'Morning Mister.
Will ⎭

Walter Will. Edward.

Will No Tom yet.

Walter (*covering up*) He's here. He's with the parson.

Geoffrey (*innocuously*) Have we had bells for five?

Edward We have, sir.

Will (*pointedly*) We've had bells for quarter past five.

Geoffrey Really? Well, the parson hears a confession yet but he'll be along shortly. Walter can get you going. (*Ominously*) There are a change or two this year.

Will We're due breakfast, Mister.

Geoffrey Has that not come neither?

Will No. Neither.

Geoffrey I'll see to it.

Will Please, Mister.

Geoffrey Completely forgot.

Will Mister: we heard speak of more pageant pence wanted.

Geoffrey (*defensively*) I know. These plays is costing the Guilds a fortune. I know, lads. A penny's a lot. *I* can't spare a penny just so. Not like some: sitting on their arses on the dry land while a ship sails making them a fortune. No, I'm opposed to more pageant pence, me. There's talk of sharing our play with the Masons.

Will (*outraged*) Never!

Edward (*outraged*) What!

Geoffrey Oh aye! And I'm the one who's talking! Aye! These pageants is nothing but a pestilence in my opinion. An excuse for time off and clowning about.

Will (*offended*) *Five* morning we rehearse, Mister. And that off our wage.

Geoffrey We has more feast days in this country than work days.

Walter (*conciliatorily*) We should get going lads. There's new words for us all.

Geoffrey No use moaning to me, Will. I've got cakes and ale to dole out. I've got pullers to pay. I've got lights to buy. I've got a mask to leaf in gold. How much is that costing? (*He looks to Walter*)

Edward We all contribute.

Geoffrey To me, see: I'm no reveller ... these days is just Christ done mischief to above the wagon and more mischief done underneath. Half the watchers pissed or sleeping or feeling each other. There's more thought of whoring than of God.

Walter (*shrewdly*) Last year it were reckoned our pageant was finest played.

Geoffrey (*egotistically*) Oh aye. I know that. It were reckoned we were a bull among bullocks!

Will (*cockily*) We were.

Geoffrey I know that. I know that. But we has to save money, Walter. It is as Will says, many things come before a play.

Will (*wounded again*) Never said that! 'Tis our play and we'll not lose it for the sake of a penny.

Geoffrey Then be careful not to lose it for the sake of complaining. (*Sternly*) Now I wants reckoning of savings to take back to the Guild, Walter.

Walter Aye, Mister.

Geoffrey Else these plays is cancelled. That's my mind spoke. So. And bid the priest come see me sharpish. (*He makes to exit*) 'Morning, lads.

All 'Morning, Mister.

Geoffrey exits

Will (*as soon as Geoffrey is out of earshot*) "I can't spare a penny just so!" His bed cost twenty pound!

Edward You shouldn't grumble so, Will. Makes matters worse.

Will Why? Because he threatens us? He can't cut our play. The sky would fall on his head. What would they do, eh? Miss out the crucifixion? Ach!

Walter No, they'd give it to the Merchants.

Will Every year we hear the same story; 'tis to keep our hands tied behind us.

Edward One minute you moan about more money; the next about less.

Will Aye, I do! 'Tis a duty to play the play. And even if God would forgive us the town would not.

Walter An' I tell you, the Merchants would take our pageant and no-one would protest, except us.

Will Except us. US would be sufficient! Don't give us the master's view, Mister Apprentice. We know it.

Edward Leave off, Will.

Will Well.

Edward Thing is, Walter, me and Will and the others . . . Tom . . . we done this pageant years, see. Just the thought of playing her warms cold fingers in January . . . beats the heart come Spring. It's our occasion, in't it?

Walter (*hurt*) I love the play no less than you do.

Edward Course you do.

Will (*knowing this, but still grumpy*) What changes anyway?

Walter They've cut the end business with the purple cloak.

Will And why's that?

Walter Too long. Been complaints to the council about running time. It's reckoned that all forty-eight plays got to be seen within the day, including the Mass.

Edward Not possible.

Walter I know it, Edward, but just the same we cut some. Besides, then we pays less for lights—if we're shorter . . . and if you lose the dividing-up of the cloak that's a purple cloth saved.

Will Ach! Saved! We know what's saved, nipper. 'Tis what's lost is the bugger. These pageant masters would be masters of no pageant at all left up to them. Yet they're never so happy while they can hoof ahead of us, all plush with our banner. Great galleybagging gang.

Edward Don't yoppel on so, Will.

Walter They also want less of the soldiers early on.

Will Do they! What about less Mary?

Walter No. There's less Mary already.

Will (*caustically*) Oh aye! And not because you're groomed for pageant master. We can all clot, Mister. You clot with that lot, please yourself. We'll clot together.

Walter I would do less Mary, Will. I'd do *no* Mary and something else, given the chance. I do have a beard now. (*He feels it*) Some. And I'm betrothed. I long to act in hose and not in petticoat. But I don't choose that neither. I play the Virgin and you play less soldier. There: view the changes.

Will You know I don't know letters. None of us do.

Edward I know some. I know E for Edward and Y for Young and P for Pinner and some others.

Will I'm talking about reading, Edward, and you can't. Nor can any of us saving Mr Walter here.

Walter I'll learn you your parts and we'll do well.

Edward That's kind, Walter.

Walter You making blood yet, Will?

Will I done it a week ago.

Edward Looks marvellous real. You'd think he'd bled himself. And I made new pins.

Walter This year our pageant's having a fresh face for Christ. I'm making him. A quarter ounce of silver in it.

Edward I could eat off that whole winter. Longer.

Will Still. It's the Lord's face. Should be special.

Walter Amen.

Edward Amen.

Walter So. We're starting. You each had five speeches before Christ had his.

Will (*showing all his fingers*) Then ten and I call on company to lift the cross.

Walter No, hold up, Will. Now Thomas speaks once only for Christ and that at the end. So where he spoke first he now says nothing and you continue but lose your speech before he spoke and after. You with me?

Edward So, we says five and then straight away ten and then company?

Walter No, you says four and then nine and then company.

Will (*grumpily*) 'Tis irregular now though, ain't it? 'Cause I used to have one hand's worth beforehand and two hands' worth after.

Edward Always were irregular, 'cause I always used to say four lines then you would say two lines and . . .

Will And different counts. (*Muttering*) It's a bugger if you ask me. 'Tis buggered up for no good reason.

Edward Oh, I think 'tis a nice touch to have the Christ dumb until the end.

Will Edward, you'd thank a bugger for bashing you!

Walter (*delicately*) Do get more complex later, Edward, to tell you the truth.

Edward (*maudlin*) Oh.

Will (*grumpily*) Aye: Bloody oh!

Father Henry Melton, the Chaplain and producer, enters with Thomas

Father Melton Have I missed the breakfast?

Walter No Father, it comes yet.

Father Melton 'Tis a real penance the Lord sent me: hunger. I hunger through the night like no other man I know.

Walter We begun, Father, we're learning changes.

Father Melton Splendid. I've made alterations lads, to improve the speeches. And 'tis also shorter. If a thing is worth talking about for two minutes 'tis better said in one. And in plain words, in English.

Walter I've touched on the differences, Father.

Father Melton Aye. 'Tis the picture speaks, in my view. Not the words. Oh yes. So I'm sad about losing the cloth, me, and the dice. The masters tell me 'tis an expense and not necessary. (*He shrugs*) And Walter, do you still speak for the Virgin? You have increasingly a beard.

Walter I do, Father, but I'll scrape it shortly.

Father Melton Were it to me, I'd have a girl say it, no offence. A girl were chosen for the deed, a girl should say it. The Blessed Mary were a beauty and what we get instead is a dozen youth with small beard and piping voice. Still, the masters would cut the pageant and the Archbishop would stop it altogether. So, Walter, you're preferred to nothing.

Walter Thank you, Father.

Father Melton See, left to me I'd never show Christ wounded. No, I'd take a strapping lad and paint his whole flesh gold, not just the face alone, and have him golden, transcendent on the tree in majesty. So come the great speech, he'd slip the nails and rope and stand arms stretched in blessing, not in pain. (*Acting his fantasy*) "Ah Father, forgive them their cruelty. They know nothing of me. They here have me tree'd. For Adam's sin I now bleed ..." and so forth. But the taste is for mumbling and hurt and violence and cruelty.

Thomas, of course, couldn't be less appropriate for this vision. He's middle-aged and fat

Edward But surely, Pastor, if we show not Christ's suffering, how can we teach men to sorrow at it and seek forgiveness?

Father Melton Ach. The world is swollen with suffering and sorrow. I've seen enough of it. Still, let's begin and do the moves alone. All the bashing and the bother. Get yourself on the tree now, Tom. I want to show the soldiers the new moves.

Edward How do, Thomas?

Edward helps Thomas to the cross

Thomas (*cautiously*) Oh. Fair.

Edward (*to Will*) Looks a bit wan, don't he, Will?

Will (*mischievously*) 'Tis that new young wife of his: tiring him out. Looks older'n me now.

Thomas I *am* older'n you.

Will Aye, but you never looked it before. This year you do.

Walter comes across to help get Tom on the cross

(*To Walter, wearily*) New moves and all now, is it?

*The three men rope Thomas to the cross which is propped up so as to keep
Thomas visible. During this*

Will I can remember when there were four soldiers, me. Each year they
takes something away. Soon they'll have the Christ crucifying hisself and
no soldiers at all.

Walter (*having had enough of Will*) You see one bird, it's a flock, ain't it
Will?

Will Maybe. What do one spot of rain signal to you? Signal a thousand to
me. All this to-do. 'Tis bad token. 'Tis bees out of a hole.

Edward Here come our breakfast, lads.

Father Melton Thank the Lord for that.

*Sarah Zachary, Thomas's wife, waiting-woman for the Le Kolves and one-
time sweetheart of Walter, enters. She's loaded up with the cakes (breadcakes) and beer*

Father Melton walks towards Sarah

How do, Sarah? Do you bring our beer? Bless you. Jump down then
Thomas, and eat.

Sarah How do, lads. Is it hungry work crucifying?

Will 'Tis mistress. Particular we eat an hour after we should.

Sarah (*sweetly, to her husband*) Can I help you, husband?

Thomas (*half-crucified but cheerful*) No. I manage. Do you, with that
weight? (*Meaning the jug of beer, etc.*)

Sarah Aye.

*Sarah moves across to Walter as the group settles down to breakfast and
Thomas disentangles himself from the cross*

Sarah Walter.

Walter Sarah.

Sarah And how is it with you, sir?

Walter I'm well, mistress. An' you?

Sarah Aye.

Walter Fair enough.

Sarah We heard you was betrothed then.

Walter Aye.

Sarah Eleanor dell Brigg. That's a good match for you, Walter.

Walter Aye. They say so.

Sarah I'm glad then. And you've got a little beard.

Walter Aye. A little.

Will (*facetiously*) Going to rub off that fluff, make a paint brush, eh
Walter?

Sarah (*to Walter*) I has to measure you for your new dress.

Walter (*uncomfortably*) Not drinking, Thomas?

Thomas Will do.

Edward You are queer quiet, Thomas.

Thomas (*mindful of Sarah and Walter*) Ngh.

Edward You sickening?

Thomas No.

Will Done hisself an injury on the planks.

Walter Have some cakes.

Will I heard say at Beverley last year, from John Lunn, that their Christ on the Pinners' pageant got hisself crucified real. Hung him up like a hare they did. He couldn't get his breath. They thought he were pretending but he weren't. Couldn't tell see, under his mask.

Edward Poor nipper.

Will Oh aye, and at Coventry they didn't care much for their boy and thumped in the nails right through his hands.

Thomas Never!

Will Ah! So you *have* still got your tongue.

Thomas They never did!

Will So 'tis said.

Thomas Did they, Parson?

Father Melton Take no notice, Thomas.

Thomas I bet they never.

Walter Come and eat, Thomas.

Sarah Thomas Zachary, you're an old donkey if you listen to this gang. Dip your nose in the jug, lovely, and shut up.

Thomas sulks across

Kathryn Le Kolve appears

(*Jumping up*) Mistress!

Kathryn How do.

The Men jump up

No. Don't stand on ceremony, lads. I needs a word apart with the priest. 'Morning Walter. How goes the rehearsal?

Walter (*wearily*) Very punctuated, madam.

Kathryn How's that?

Walter As yet it has few starts and many stops.

Kathryn Aye well: proceed. Proceed. Can they proceed, Parson?

Father Melton I fear they waits on me, madam.

Kathryn Then come apart, quick. (*She pulls the priest aside*)

Father Melton (*as Kathryn pulls him away*) Point out the changes, Walter.

There are frustrated looks from the actors at a further hiatus. They pack up their breakfast during what follows

Kathryn (*unburdening her news immediately*) Henry, I heard the Earl of Oxford came last night to stop at the Mayor's house.

Father Melton Oxford? Impossible. He's exiled.

Kathryn Not by the King.

Father Melton The King agreed it.

Kathryn He says the King comes here.

Father Melton You emerge too early from your bed, Kathryn.

Kathryn He says the King will be here this morning. And Queen. And retinue.

Father Melton Why?

Kathryn The King is sullen with London, is the word.

Father Melton His Majesty is a man of culture. Why should he come here? No, 'tis idle this rumour. (*Conscious of the others*) Be with you directly, lads.

Kathryn (*undeterred*) And what if the King came to be with the Earl? 'Tis said that when Oxford were at court he could make Richard see black as white and white as black.

Father Melton (*excited*) Would it were true. Would spice the town.

Kathryn I'm off to spice myself.

Father Melton My God, Kathryn. I hope he stop for the pageant and like mine. I'd give my splinter from the true cross for some gold paint and good cloth and even half good players. Oh Christ! He might bring me to court and I could give up scratching about here.

Walter Should we do the moves, Parson?

Father Melton Aye, do the moves.

Bells ring severally and noisily

Thomas
Edward } (*together*) Yow!

Edward What's this!

All react

Will Christ's blood! Them jangle! What's up, then?

Edward Told you, Will. That heron! 'Tis bad luck, I bet! 'Tis a famine!

Walter What bells are these, Parson?

Father Melton What bells? They're all the bells!

Walter Aye, but what do they signify?

Father Melton I don't know, boy.

Kathryn (*delighted*) I think it may be the King coming!

All The King!

Kathryn Aye.

Will (*shouting at the bells*) Why?

Edward Never heard so many bells.

Will All right we heard!

Geoffrey runs in, yelling over the tumult

Geoffrey (*shouting*) The King comes! The King comes!

The bells stop

(*Still shouting*) The King comes!

Kathryn Aye, husband, they know.

Geoffrey How do they know?

Kathryn I told them.

Geoffrey How do you know, madam?

Kathryn (*dissembling*) Oh. (*Meaning, never you mind*)

Geoffrey (*deflated*) Don't just gawp, nippers. There's no rehearsal now.

We're out at the gates to greet the Royal Party. Get to, Walter. The Mayor's craft is half way there.

Kathryn They can't go dressed so.

Geoffrey No. You can't go dressed so. Go and change into Sunday outfit and fetch our banner.

Walter and Will exit

Shift that cross, Thomas, Edward. Don't dawdle! You're all dawdling! Come on, come on! 'Tis a race not a funeral! Let's meet directly by Mickelgate.

Kathryn Sarah, go back to the house and pull out my maroon gown. It needs spicing.

Father Melton (*excited*) I'll hurry, too. I've a sword to buckle on and 'tis a chance to wear my new cross from Venice. I'll see you both at Mickelgate.

Father Melton exits

Geoffrey (*sourly*) That priest is a penance.

Kathryn He's nothing of the sort. He can read. And he forgives me. 'Tis two things *you* can't do. At least.

Geoffrey Ach! And what do this King want now? Christ! 'Tis one trial after another. And how is it, woman, you know the business of the town before I do?

Kathryn I listens, sir. You spend so much time talking. If you want to know, I heard the King is in sulk with London.

Geoffrey How in sulk?

Kathryn For respecting not His Majesty.

Geoffrey Ah! 'Tis a money thing then.

Kathryn Some others say the King love this Oxford more than his wife.

Geoffrey Woman, most men love most men more than their wife.

Kathryn Oh?

Geoffrey Not me. I kiss your finger, madam, and if your foot came more often to my bed I would kiss that also.

Kathryn I hate your bed. It's straw.

Geoffrey Then let me come to yours.

Kathryn With my maid at the foot of it? 'Tis not seemly.

Geoffrey For my part I would throw out the maid.

Kathryn For my part you should throw out the bed, sir, and find a new one more suitable. That's the remedy.

Geoffrey Madam, I spend twenty pounds on your bed because of your horror of the straw one. Now I has the straw one.

Kathryn Aye, husband. That's true.

Geoffrey Well ... ach, Christ's blood!

Kathryn Where do we greet the King, sir?

Geoffrey By Ouse Bridge.

Kathryn Oh no! Not me. That bridge stinks and I'll not sniff it.

Geoffrey It does not stink.

Kathryn You have no nose, husband, how would you know? If you would buy me parfum I could travel more. I could smell myself and not the foul

air. I will not walk neither. You may be happy to greet a King with skirts
beshitted. I am not.

Geoffrey Madam, I am not in charge of the whole town and cannot be
blamed for it.

Kathryn But I do not blame you for the whole town but simply for *not* being
in charge of it. Run ahead now, and arrange horses and a better view.
(*Thinking*) If a King comes, profit comes in his train. Run!

Geoffrey huffs

But not sweatily, sir!

Geoffrey Ach.

Geoffrey exits unhappily. Then Kathryn exits, happily

SCENE 2

The Mayor's house

*This is the bedroom or upper storey. There is a shuttered space rather than a
window*

*In the room Richard II, his Queen, Anne of Bohemia, and the exiled Earl,
Robert de Vere of Oxford, are reunited. Richard is embracing Oxford*

Richard Robert!

Oxford Richard! Anne! Marvellous.

Anne (*concerned*) Robert, you're grey.

Oxford (*shrugging*) Dust. (*Concerned*) You're thin.

Anne (*tightly*) I don't think so.

Richard When did you come? Yesterday?

Oxford Aye. Last evening.

Anne Let's not go down. Let's stay up here and talk.

Richard There's a feast done for us.

Anne (*mischievously*) Say I sicken.

Oxford Oh do, please, Majesty. The people here will speak French and
cannot. I want to speak English. I would not care if I never heard a
bonjour or a *bonsoir* before purgatory. Tell me of London.

Richard No.

Anne He hates London now, Robert. Without you. Without friends.
Without money.

Oxford Is it bad?

Richard Worse. The city vomits merchants and lawyers. The court con-
spires. Gloucester and Bolingbroke torment me. London's piss drowns
me.

Anne (*sadly*) I cannot conceive there, Robert. I lost two babies since we last
spoke.

Richard The Parliament would speak my words for me, move my hands like
so. (*He demonstrates a puppet*) They call me weak because I love not
warmongering and the endless bloodying.

Oxford And because you once loved Oxford.

Richard Still do, friend.

Oxford Oh, London still sounds like heaven after Calais and Bordeaux and those puddles of nowhere, Sire. Not a sun but I thought of you, not a laugh but I heard yours, not a game but I saw you play it, not a pageant but I remembered your hurrah.

Richard No laughs now, Robert, nor games. London is loveless.

Oxford Then it is you who is London in my heart and now London is in York with Oxford.

Anne And Bohemia.

Oxford And Bohemia!

Richard I kicked out the Mayor at home, Robert, and his crew, and they can linger on my pleasure.

Oxford Bravo.

Richard It were never meant for tradesmen to govern. It is against God that a King should be worked from below.

Oxford But what do you hope for here?

Anne Rest.

Richard Give them a few weeks, the fat cats will purr for me again. Meanwhile, we three can live a little out of time.

Anne We might move the court here if it pleases us.

Oxford I only fear that this place is more of the same. The Mayor here is so full of Mayor he cannot squeeze into his gown an inch of wit.

Richard He bowed and scraped an hour outside the gates until I fell asleep on his speech. We waded here, Robert. Half the town oozing on us.

Oxford And the Mayoress is inflated. Like a pig's bladder for football. She knows nothing but insists on revealing it.

Anne This is a fine bed.

Richard Anne judges each new place by its bed.

Anne I do. This bed is a better bed than ours, Richard.

Oxford Ask them for it. They can't refuse.

Richard I might.

Oxford It will flatter them you want their beds. Each will out-peacock the other until they realize that to show off so they must lose what they most prize: the thing. 'Tis a people of thing, these guildsmen.

Anne What "thing"?

Oxford A "thing". Any "thing". Beds, bolsters, pisspots, conduits, baubs, trinkets, hangings ... anything. What breeding they lack inside they disguise in this weight of thing. They even die now and have these things buried with them.

Richard You've not changed, Robert.

Oxford Demand these things. That what they own is coveted is essential to their design ... that a King wants them is marvellous. They'll bestow them on you flushed with conceit and next flushed with anxiety. They know the worth of each thing down to the last farthing and will cost out their generosity tear by tear.

Richard This polemic cost you your land, your fortune and London's favour.

Oxford Good riddance then, eh?

Anne And you have one rule for your friends and another for the world.

Oxford Who has not? I hate the pig with power, the donkey with degree. I hate books unread and songs unheard and glass unviewed and all beauty wasted. And I talk too much.

Anne You do, and I love it.

Richard And I do.

Anne I'll have the bed. The colour suits me. I think I'll lie down on it, too. Come boys and cosset me.

Richard Do you know this woman has been sick, Oxford?

Oxford How sick?

Richard She swoons on me and fevers on me and coughs and chokes and spasms on me. No thought of my peace. (*Gently*) Is that not so, madam?

Anne I'm inconsiderate.

Richard January she even feigned death to grieve me. (*He clasps Anne's hand*)

Oxford (*clasping Anne's other hand*) Hussy.

Anne I know.

Richard And dead babes she hands me, just so.

Oxford Wicked.

Anne 'Tis too many eyes on me, Robert, none friendly.

Oxford Then we will make of this a season of sport to cure us all.

Richard Amen.

Anne To mischief!

Oxford To mischief!

Richard To mischief!

Oxford (*only half believing what he says*) And surely come the autumn: London, starved of majesty, will embrace you.

Anne And we can bring you back in our train.

Oxford I like this scheme.

Richard Robert, what of the play here? How is it?

Oxford Good, I hear.

Richard If it rivals Coventry 'tis the one thing the country does to out-art London.

Anne Richard, show him your wipe.

Oxford What's this?

Richard My wipe!

Oxford I'm lost.

Richard produces a large handkerchief and blows his nose

Ha!

Richard hands it to Anne who blows hers

Richard Robert

Robert blows his nose. He laughs

It saves the sleeve, eh?

They grin hugely

Oxford Whose invention is this?

Anne Richard's.

Oxford 'Tis very strange.

Richard How strange! 'Tis very wondrous! I have many and use them variously: one for the nose; one for the arse; one for the brow.

Anne An' he mix them up.   •

Oxford True. 'Tis very wondrous.

Richard Here, (*he fishes around and produces half a dozen handkerchiefs*) try them.

Anne The Parliament call him woman for this hygiene.

Oxford I call them shit flies for theirs!

Richard To women then!

Oxford And away with shit flies.

Anne Away with them!

SCENE 3

The Mayor's house. A room below

The Mayor and Mayoress wait to eat and wonder how you tell a King he's late for dinner

Alice What transpires up there, husband?

William I don't know.

Alice They won't have servants in with them. That's unnatural.

William How unnatural?

Alice Well, 'tis not done, is it?

William What the King do becomes what's done, madam.

Alice True. *Je ne sais pas*. The Earl of Oxford is exceeding strange, though.

William Aye.

Alice whispers confidential rumours about Oxford's exploits

Why whisper, wife, when we're alone?

Alice Such things should not be shouted. (*She whispers some more*)

William Well, I don't know, do I? They come from London and have different customs.

Alice Should we learn them, then?

William An' they're Kings! (*Thinking*) I don't know. What I do know is I'm hungered and my belly rumbles and churns and can sniff the table.

Alice We can't eat until they come down. The Queen has bathed herself. And the King. Is that the fashion too? To come in from outdoors and wash the body?

William I don't know.

Alice I'm certain the physic would say it risks sickness ... but if it be the fashion we should do it, husband, and encourage the town.

William Woman, I am already the laughing stock with all this hygiene law you make me champion.

Alice 'Tis the smell of pig particular offends me.

William Never used to.

Alice And Kathryn Le Kolve told she read in a book that in Italy they have a law against *any* slops in the street.

William Madam ... think for one second, pray ... if you cannot pour out the slops onto the street, what do you do with it?

Alice can't think of an answer to this argument

Alice Well she said the Italians have a law against it.

William (*sulky*) I'll not strip my clothes every day; it's a business.

Alice Aye. Well. His Majesty have a cloth, too. He use it most mysteriously. Wiping. Hm. I suppose I could have some made up.

William Madam ... eight shillings of mutton and venison and capon rot on our table while we prattle on about the fashion of arses—whether we should poke them or wash them or wipe them. For me I want food in my gut so as to do with my arse what God made it for and I will continue to slop out its product until God or you show me a way of magically vanishing it.

Alice (*placating*) William ...

William What?

Alice strokes William

Stop it.

Alice Willum ... Willum ...

William Whatee?

Alice We has a King and Queen in our house, husband.

William I know.

Alice The town be green.

William I know.

Alice So green—Kathy Le Kolve will sicken with greenness.

William And the husband.

Alice They'll be so green they dare not walk the pastures less a cow graze on them.

William (*proudly*) Always stayed before in the Castle or the Abbey. Always.

Alice Get this noted in the record book then; tonight a King and Queen sleep in the bed of William and Alice Selby.

William Our bed?

Alice Where else?

William Where do we sleep?

Alice I'm to my mother's house and you down with your sons.

William With the dogs and the rabble?

Alice You'll not die of it. Oh, and we must buy music, too. This King loves music.

William Why buy? Can't we invite someone over?

Alice That's no use. He must have proper minstrels. Leave it with me.

William Ach! It don't feel good all this cost.

Alice Listen, husband, you have twenty cases at law.

William Twenty-four.

Alice Well then, get the King's favour and think on it.

William No, twenty-five now I remember.
Alice Think, too, on *Sir* William Selby.
William Sir William. Sir Will.
Alice Lady Alice.
William My Lady.
Alice My Lord.
William What—my Lady?
Alice Oh. (*Mock sigh*) Nothing, my Lord.

They dance gleefully. Then eventually William pulls up

William By Christ that flesh smells good.
Alice I know. It do. Let's go up, eh?

SCENE 4

The Mayor's house. The bedroom

Anne, Richard and Oxford are sprawled on the bed

William (*off*) Majesty? Majesties?
Oxford 'Tis the dog after his dinner.
William (*off*) Majesties . . .
Richard Should we stay a-bed and scandalize them?
Oxford Aye. Let's.
William (*off*) Majesties.
Alice (*off*) His Worship the Mayor and Lady Mayoress approach the Royal Salon.
Oxford (*mock impressed*) Salon!
Richard *Entrez.*

 William and Alice enter

William We *entrez maintenant*, Your Most Shining Radiance.
Alice Forgive this *petite* intrusion.
Richard *Nous sommes ici, madame. Au lit.*

Alice tries not to look surprised

Alice Pardon?
Richard (*very swiftly*) *Parce que vous vous dandinez en parlant le francais, j'ai pensé, faussement, que vous compreniez la langue et désiriez la parler avec nous.*
Alice (*lost*) Um . . . pardon?
William (*hungry and very lost*) The thing is, my Lord, the feast cools and the flies visit the table before we do.
Anne Ugh!
Richard My wife sickens, Mayor, and would eat in our "salon".
William Uh . . .
Alice Of course, Your Majestic . . . uh . . . Majesty.
Richard What is the fare?

Alice Capons ... mutton ... venison ... small bird, sturgeon, pike.

Anne 'Tis excessive, madam.

Alice Uh ...

William 'Tis in your honour, Your Shining Beacons.

Anne Do you not have poor in the town?

Alice We do, ma'am.

Anne Good, then they should taste of this feast, in our honour. Say the King and his Queen wish to thank the citizens for their gracious hospitality. That is our pleasure.

William (*distraught*) Distribute it to the poor, glorious Lady?

Anne Aye. It should go out to the streets this minute. In truth the stench of it poisons my nostrils somewhat. (*Innocently*) Have you ate?

William No, no, we waited on you, sweet Queen.

Anne Shame. Still, fasting's good for choler.

William Does our feast not please you, glorious Majesty?

Anne Oh yes, it do. Most sincere.

Oxford What pleases the Queen more, sir, is this bed.

Anne Marvellous bed.

Oxford And the King like it.

Richard Very fine bed.

Anne (*to Richard*) I'd like the bed, sir. Might I not have one like it?

Richard 'Tis not mine to give, Lady. Though were it I'd delight in bestowing it on you.

William (*miserably*) 'Tis mine, madam, no *were* mine and now 'tis yours.

Anne No. Surely not!

Alice Oh yes, gracious Sovereign, 'tis our joy to gift it.

Anne Then I'm happy now. And like this place which hitherto I liked not much.

Richard (*explaining*) The Queen find too much air in here.

Anne Oh? Do I?

Richard You do, madam.

Anne I do.

Alice One could draw the canopy, sire, and shelter from any draught. 'Tis what I do.

Richard How, mistress?

Alice Like so. (*Struggling with the bed canopy*) Help, William.

William Aye. Beg pardon.

William and Alice draw the curtains half round the bed

Richard Do they not surround us, then?

William Can do. Can do.

Richard Then do. Then do.

William and Alice curtain the bed off by means of the canopy. The King, Queen and Oxford are now completely hidden. William and Alice exchange glances. They don't know what to do next. There's a pause. Then William coughs

William Majesty?

Richard Aye? What is it?
William Do you want else?
Richard How else?
William I don't know, sire. Just else.
Richard No.
William Should we leave you then, O Brightest Stars in the Firmament?
Richard As you wish.
Alice We will stay Lord, if you require it.
Richard (*conferring*) Do we require it?
Anne Not overly.
Richard (*out*) Not overly. Just as you like.

William and Alice exchange uneasy and embarrassed glances, becalmed and confused. From inside the canopy, a giggle

SCENE 5

A room in the house of Geoffrey and Kathryn Le Kolve

Geoffrey Le Kolve paces about, agitated. Sitting are Kathryn and Father Henry Melton. They're eating an elaborate meal

Geoffrey I'll tell you what will happen.
Kathryn Oh?
Geoffrey He'll petition the King. That's what. Mark this. That's what he'll do.
Kathryn To what end?
Geoffrey For my land down Hen Street. Two houses. He's had me in court twice over it and been thrown out. Now he'll petition the King.
Kathryn Oh, them! What do you say? Two houses? Two huts you mean, barely stood up. Where you put Thomas and Sarah.
Geoffrey Two labourers' houses.
Kathryn You don't want them huts, husband. And Thomas could go to your house in Bootham. That's bigger. And empty.
Geoffrey I do want 'em! An' I should be Mayor, too. It's my turn. He been Mayor three years. I should be Mayor! Then the King would sleep at our house and I could petition him about my quarrel over them five acres in Stamford Bridge. An' I promised the Bootham house to Walter. So I do want 'em!
Kathryn Ease up, husband. You'll be sick.
Geoffrey I am sick. (*To Father Melton*) I prayed over them acres, Pastor; a lot of good it done me.
Father Melton Pray? How?
Geoffrey How? Rosary. Um ... Novenas. I don't know—plain prayers ... "Dear God, let me have that land" prayers. Amen.
Father Melton For prayers re: land you need a relic of some sort. Let me think ... Uh! A piece of St Peter's keys. They'll unlock property.
Geoffrey Aye?

Father Melton I have a piece, but 'tis not cheap.

Geoffrey To buy?

Father Melton To kiss. I'll not sell relics. 'Tis corrupt.

Geoffrey An' 'tis bad business.

Kathryn To think that Alice Selby entertains a King and Queen. It makes me boil.

Geoffrey And me.

Kathryn Her kitchen's no comparison with mine. Nor her cooks. Nor her hangings. Nor her bed. *And* it's small that house.

Geoffrey Oh, 'tain't small.

Kathryn 'Tis small. The building is big out but 'tis not big indoors. What do you say, Henry?

Father Melton Um. I'm not worldly on the size of houses.

Kathryn 'Tis good you should have one thing to be not worldly on.

Father Melton I think so.

Kathryn Worse, the woman herself is big outside but small indoors. She buys books and talks a sort of French and understands neither.

Geoffrey You set too much store by books, madam. She's a good wife, that mistress. She been more Mayor than him.

Kathryn Oh has she? And have *I* not been *your* back legs for twenty year?

Geoffrey She's seen at functions.

Kathryn (*outraged*) And I am seen, sir! And I am seen! I guarantee I am seen at functions *more* even if I attend fewer. Men have washed up at my bosom, Mister. More fellows shipwrecked on me than Alice Selby have anchored with her leaden chat at your precious functioning. Is that not the truth, Father?

Father Melton Oh. Uh. 'Tis probable.

Geoffrey A man cannot succeed public when his private is wagged from tongue to tongue.

Kathryn (*in mock outrage*) And what mean you by that, prithee?

Geoffrey (*backing down*) I should be Mayor, that's all.

Kathryn Now you take heed, Mister. I'll not be scape-goat to your thin blood which has more water in it than you cheat into your paint.

Geoffrey Enough, woman!

Father Melton I have counsel could I get a word in edgeways.

Kathryn What?

Father Melton 'Tis simple. Speak to the King yourself. Gain audience. Take gifts. Kathryn will charm him. She has made walls smile; a King should not trouble her. Honeyed so, he will hear your case no less kindly than the Mayor's.

Kathryn Better, I should speak to the wife. She has no children. I'll cure that.

Father Melton No witchery, madam. It's a mortal sin.

Kathryn Herbs and good prayer, Father. Not witchery.

Geoffrey So you think we should present ourselves? Hmm? At the Mayor's house?

Father Melton If needs be. Course, if the King stop for the Feast day and sees the plays and like ours . . .

Kathryn But where would he watch from? Minster Gates?

Father Melton Oh no. Above the Common Hall, surely.

Geoffrey No. 'Tis uncomfortable there for so long and late in the order. (*Pessimistically*) No, no doubt he'll stop in Selby's house to watch, and hurrah their pageant and give them my land and champion their Guild and make him Mayor for life and "Rise, Sir William" and all is utter lost and useless.

Kathryn Aye, well that be positive, husband.

Geoffrey Well . . .

Kathryn First, he could watch the plays elsewhere. Second, he could like your play best. Is it best?

Geoffrey Well . . .

Kathryn Henry?

Father Melton 'Tis cheapest.

Geoffrey Never!

Father Melton 'Tis cheap.

Kathryn (*Machiavellian*) Aye, and this King love a good pageant. 'Tis a sorrow.

Geoffrey (*bristling*) You could cover our wagon with gold and Will Blue-front and them boys would still look cheap! Great galleybaggers! With their thick tongues and yoppeling.

Father Melton (*despairing*) Aye. And a fuzz-faced Mary and a fat Christ and the best bits hacked off as saving. Let me have cloth, sir! And gold!

Kathryn And change the boys, Geoffrey! If you cannot catch a King on the Cross play . . . aye . . . shoo off the old crew. That's the thing. Walter'll help. Give him the Jesus. He can soft soap the whole business.

Geoffrey (*sulkily*) I don't know.

Kathryn Would scare the back legs off the Mayor and his shrew . . .

Father Melton That's true.

Geoffrey (*thawing*) I can't afford to be throwing my money away. Each shilling I make has my sweat on it.

Kathryn Aye but 'tis not what you have, chicken, but what you can be *seen* to have. Put your money on the planks and it will be seen!

Geoffrey And what if they don't stop? And go home? Then what?

Kathryn They'll stop. They must. Do it, husband and let them hurrah your pageant and give you the Mayor and give you the land and "Rise, *Sir* Geoffrey!" And all is not lost and utter useless.

Father Melton Bravo.

Kathryn (*going to the shuttered window*) We has a stopping place outside. We has a view up here. Besides a King up here would put twenty pound on the benefit of the station. We'll win his favour and flatter his love of the play with our wagon and (*she looks out suddenly and is startled*) Husband, am I lunatic or is weird scenes going on at the Selby house?

Father Melton What's afoot?

Kathryn Come, both of you! Is that not the Mayor's house and is that not a feast being fed to paupers?

Father Melton (*sorrowfully*) My God, look at them meats.

Geoffrey By Christ, there's ten shilling on them plates. Look at them trays. Mutton.

Father Melton Sturgeon. Venison. Is that venison? I love a hung venison.
Geoffrey The blessed Virgin Mary, Mother of God. It's a madness.
Father Melton What a terrible waste. (*Miserably*) Quails.
Kathryn (*a sudden epiphany*) Husband! Quick! Quick!
Geoffrey What?
Kathryn Call the servants. We must get busy.
Geoffrey What's this?
Kathryn (*pacing*) We've got beef hung for the feast day and two lamb. It's a tragedy but I suppose the cidered ham must go and all.
Geoffrey What's this? Go where?
Kathryn Call John, quick. And Susan and Sarah and get them doling out before we lose everything ...
Geoffrey Woman, are you queer?
Father Melton What ails you, Kathryn?
Kathryn Oh, shit. I'll do it myself. I fight a lone war without a man near me with a bean to rattle in his skull. (*Wearily, as if addressing two children*) If the Mayor dole out food can only be because the King wills it. Therefore we must dole out food an' all, else we lag behind. Do you see? Now get to. (*Calling*) Sarah! Sarah!

Kathryn runs off

SCENE 6

The Streets

Alice Selby and her waiting woman; the Queen and hers; the two servants behind at some distance

Alice is exhausted from this unfamiliar walking

Alice If Your Majesty tires we could have the horses brought up.
Anne Madam, I get sore rump from riding and a joggled view of a place. I walk for my health and pleasure.
Alice (*mournfully*) Oh yes, I love a walk. An' you thirst not, Highness?
Anne I thirst for people, mistress. Do you have none in the town?
Alice People? Oh aye, we do, many. My husband thought you'd wish the streets clear.
Anne Why?
Alice We have the usual harvest of lepers and paupers. They affect the view. Also six sergeant run ahead, ma'am, sweeping the walk and shooing beggars. Did the Minster please you, my Lady? 'Tis said if our spire soared taller 'twould tear heaven.
Anne I would like it more, mistress, if you would accompany me unaccompanied by your smell. What is it?
Alice 'Tis an orange stuck with cloves and rosemary, Majesty, it keeps off infection.
Anne No doubt, but it infects me and makes my head ache.
Alice (*throwing it high behind her*) 'Tis gone, Your Majesty. I beg pardon.

Anne No madam, beg not or you will be shooed off by your sergeants. I would like people, if only to measure your spires by.

Alice Cicely! Run ahead and tell the men to call out folk to stand against their houses. *Do* you wish any by the Minster, madam? We could return and look again with persons by it.

Anne Oh no, let's walk on, eh?

Alice 'Tis a very clean town, my Lady. We have laws for hygiene. My husband made them.

Anne What think you when the people make their own laws?

Alice (*not certain what she's supposed to think*) Um . . . how think you, Your Majesty?

Anne I have no quarrel with clean streets.

Alice Yes, my husband has achieved much as Mayor. He is out all the hours of the day and if he's not devoting his energies to the town's benefit, then he's in the court up to his girdle in litigation.

Anne Oh dear.

Alice (*transparent*) By coincident we stand by two houses here which belong rightly to my husband and are contested.

Anne Which houses?

Alice Well . . . more huts, in truth . . . these madam. But for the price of a lawyer they should be palaces. The business grieves my husband sorely.

Anne I'm sorry to hear it.

Alice Are you? Are you, Most Beneficient Majesty?

Anne Well yes . . . quite sorry.

Alice I expect you, like me, hold your man upright?

Anne I expect I do, from time to time.

Alice (*warming to her task*) And I wager . . . just like me . . . you play Virgin to his Christ.

Anne How's that, mistress?

Alice You know, my Lady: to speak to him they must first speak to me.

Anne I see.

Alice Aye, those are the two huts. And other places in dispute. 'Tis a wronged family. My husband's father died in court fighting for what was rightly his.

Anne Mistress, if I hear further woes I may weep.

Alice Then I'll shut my mouth and walk quiet.

Anne Then bless you!

Alice (*immediately*) How long may you stop with us, dear Queen?

Anne Oh, I know not. Past the plays, then I know not.

Alice Aye, but definite past the pageants then?

Anne Aye.

Alice Aye. Well, my husband's guild is most proud of its plays. 'Tis most lavish. His plans are most lavish.

Anne Your husband, madam, is wonderfully represented by you.

Alice Oh. 'Tis strange. Last night I dreamed he were Sir William. I woke with cheeks wet from tears of joy.

Anne If he is one quarter the man you describe, he should be Sir at least.

Alice (*excited*) Yes! Yes, my Queen! Were he one quarter the man! What keeps Cicely? Let me run ahead and find some folk for you to look at. Will you excuse me, dear lady?

Anne I will.

Alice *Au revoir, madame.*

Anne Yes.

Alice runs off, leaving Anne alone

Sarah Zachary appears

Hello.

Sarah Your Majesty, I was called out to be looked at.

Anne Ah, thank you, and what's your name, mistress?

Sarah Sarah, madam. Married to Thomas Zachary, labourer.

Anne Well, Sarah, would you mind if I leant on you, rather than looked at you?

Sarah No madam.

Anne So Sarah, married to Thomas Zachary, labourer, are you the Mayoress' woman?

Sarah Oh no, madam, I am in the service of the Master of the Painters' Guild.

Anne And is this your house then, there's a fuss over? (*It is*)

Sarah Don't know, madam.

Anne I think it is.

Sarah I think there may be some rivalry between the Masters in the town.

Anne I think there may be too, Sarah. Gently put. Now, do you know the route back to the Mayor's house?

Sarah I do madam, I brought you a letter there this morning from my mistress.

Anne A letter?

Sarah Aye. Inviting you to view the procession of the plays from my master's window.

Anne Hmm. Lead me back then Sarah.

As they exit

Sarah Certainly, yes madam.

Anne And tell me about your mistress, what's she like?

Sarah Lovely.

Anne Lovely? And what else?

Sarah She has some lovely gowns.

Anne and Sarah exit

Scene 7

Walter's workshop

Behind a screen Walter tries on the Mary costume while Sarah waits

Sarah How is it, Master Walter?

Walter I am grown at the shoulder since last year.

Sarah Aye.

Walter And at the stomach. 'Tis not an easy fit. (*He comes out, awkward, coy*)

Walter I pass for Mary?

Sarah I think so. (*Adjusting her dress*) Mistress Eleanor has made a man of you.

Walter (*lightly*) Then I love her for others will only make a woman of me.

Sarah (*hurt*) That is not fair, Walter!

Walter I tease you.

Sarah Well, you should not. 'Tis a raw thing.

Walter (*taken aback*) Are you not happy wife to your Tom?

Sarah I am.

Walter Well then.

Sarah All the same, you should not tease.

Walter Oh Sarah. 'Tis long gone all that. Surely?

Sarah Oh. Surely. (*Pause. Adjusting the dress*) I know you could not wed me, Walter. 'Tis one world to serve and another to be served. 'Tis not your fault.

Walter (*awkward*) Well ...

Sarah I said to Mistress Eleanor I'd stitch her clothes for the church door.

Walter She said. 'Tis generous.

Sarah And I'll make the christening gown, too.

Walter Madam you need not sew us into the sheets to show your heart.

Sarah My heart I'll sew on my sleeve, sir.

Geoffrey (*off*) Walter?

Walter In here, master.

Geoffrey (*off, nearer*) Walter?

Walter Here, sir.

Geoffrey and Father Melton enter together

Geoffrey Ah Walter. (*To Sarah*) 'Morning, Sarah. (*Then inquiringly, to Walter*) How do?

Walter I sleep not for mask-making, sir. But they're made.

Geoffrey Do the merchants come for the Herod face?

Walter Aye. 'Tis wondrous red locks they bring for it: fresh cropped.

Sarah Aye. 'Tis Edward's wife's hair. She sold it to pay for their bairn.

Walter No!

Sarah Aye.

Father Melton See, mister, they lavish on their pageant.

Sarah They do, mister. We heard they have new hose for the Jews and send for armour from Beverley.

Geoffrey Ach!

Father Melton See, Geoffrey. The boy grows too much boy for the Blessed Virgin.

Sarah I do redress the dress, Father.

Father Melton (*doubtfully*) But the face, too ...

Geoffrey Walter, the merchants will outplay us; they plan to bring in their Herod, and the Kings, and will have a maid to play the Mother.

Walter Never!

Father Melton In London, Walter, the wives play the Assumption themselves. They know the King's likings and pander. So must we.

Walter So I am dumped, then?

Geoffrey Not dumped. We'll make a Jesus of you.

Father Melton 'Tis what you will.

Sarah And Thomas?

Geoffrey We propose you to play the Mary, Sarah. You has a clear voice and fair face, and we hear the Queen smiled on you ...

Walter And Thomas?

Father Melton Our scheme is to change all the men. Not just Thomas.

Walter How change?

Father Melton We search for new soldiers and may use the players from De La Poles of Hull.

Walter Minstrels?

Geoffrey No, they play the Interludes and are highly spoke of. Will cost us eight pound.

Walter And why spend eight pound, pray, when your current men know the pageant and love it and are the pride of the Pinners and Painters?

Father Melton *Parce-que*, Walter, 'tis a play before a King.

Walter Do he not value these qualities?

Sarah I think he do.

Geoffrey Think, Mister, of the merchants' might. If we stick to our humble fare 'tis comparison of donkey with stallion.

Walter 'Tis a town, Mister, of citizens not knights, and thus have more use of donkeys. In my view.

Father Melton You wished to speak for Christ, Walter. Now you can. Your Thomas has played him too long, Sarah. 'Tis a young man's part. We all know it. And the cuts are restored. And the cloth, mistress. I have this new notion for the Christ's cloak. 'Tis so: Walter come on wrapped in the small purple. After he lay on the tree and the soldiers come to dice for it, 'tis picked up and on a sudden is lengths and lengths long.

Sarah How?

Father Melton I have method for substitution. The crowd will watch the *crucifying*, not the cloth.

Walter The business of the cloth, Parson, is similar to the business of the play. A week ago were subject to cuts, now is to be enlarged beyond belief.

Father Melton This Christ you will play, Walter, will be all gold on the planks; not simply the mask. And despite the buffeting will not be wracked but will rest transcendent on the tree while the purple cloth billows out beneath him.

Geoffrey So ...

Walter And our rehearsal?

Geoffrey Oh, rehearse! No harm done in that. Besides, Da La Poles' may not appear. No, rehearse. Don't want to upset the cart just yet, Walter.

Walter Then excuse me, Mister, pardon.

Geoffrey Aye.
Father Melton I'll follow shortly.
Sarah May I go now an' all, sir?
Geoffrey Aye, do. But be bound to say nothing to the others, now.
Sarah Aye, sir.

Walter and Sarah exit

Geoffrey and Father Melton ruminate

Father Melton Hm.
Geoffrey The girl can be replaced. 'Tis a sop, in case the Queen do like her. Walter'll do it.
Father Melton I'm not so certain.
Geoffrey Oh I am, me. He'll want to get on. Aye, well if he don't, there's plenty who will. Forget this rehearsal, Chaplain, and get word to Hull. And see if you can't get them for seven pound, eh?

Geoffrey and Father Melton exit

SCENE 8

The Mayor's gardens. A prized lawn

Richard, Oxford and William appear armed with golf clubs and balls

William (*cheerfully*) So, my Lord, what is it we aims at? (*Indicating merrily with his club offstage and up*) The Minster glass! Ha!
Oxford He swing that club elegantly, eh sire?
Richard 'Tis a sportsman.
William Well, more a Carlisle axe I'm used to.
Oxford Ah, a warrior!
William An' I like a kick at football.
Oxford 'Tis banished from London, football.
William Aye, an' here.
Oxford The traders say it disturb their stalls.
William (*uncomfortably*) Aye.
Oxford (*pointedly*) They do the same with men who disturb them.
William Aye?
Oxford (*violently*) Aye, they do. They kick 'em out. Anything which disturbs their pile of coins: out!
William So, this golf, my Lords: a case of he who sends the ball furthest, is it?
Richard Oh no, 'tis not a show of strength, Mayor, but of elegance. 'Tis one sport where brute force is not everything. No, 'tis a hole we need for a beginning.
William A hole? What kind of hole, Majesty?
Richard Oh, a small one. Here will do nicely.
William This is my green, sire. 'Tis prized.

Richard Aye, 'tis perfect for the game, Mayor. Congratulations. Have you seen a better green, Robert?

Oxford Never.

Richard Nor me. Shall we start then, or must I admire your grass further?

William (*tragically*) No. I'll just dig up a hole then. Here, you say?

Richard Don't set to yourself, Mayor. You're playing. Have a boy out with a trowel. Otherwise every time we need another hole you'll be too occupied gardening to play.

William How many of these holes do we need?

Richard As we like, Mayor. As we like.

William I'll get a boy, then. And a trowel. Excuse me, my lords.

William exits, leaving Richard and Oxford alone

The Queen enters

Anne My lords, no golf?

Richard We're due, madam. We wait on the holes.

Anne Ah. And how do the holes go down with the Mayor?

Richard Deep, madam, deep.

Oxford His heart thump so, we fear it may thump out.

Anne No matter. His wife approaches and will have him canonized directly.

William returns with a servant

William Dig here, boy.

Richard Aye lad: a hole the size of your fist and the length of your arm to the elbow.

The boy sets to work

Anne Good day, Mayor.

William Oh, Majesty, forgive me! My mind wanders.

Anne Aye, well, how could you notice me? I am not at grass level.

William No. (*Wincing at the hole*) *Enough!* (*Then anxiously to the King*) Surely?

Richard A finger more, I reckon. Eh, Robert?

Oxford Aye, a thumb.

Richard That's it. Now, Mayor. Over here and tap your ball to the hole. He who sinks his ball with least strokes, wins. You begin.

William Oh no. You must start, sire.

Richard No. You.

William I couldn't.

Richard Start!

William As Your Majesty bids. (*He makes a good putt*)

Anne Well done, Mayor!

Richard Aye, well hit! Now me. (*He makes a bad putt*)

William Good, Majesty.

Richard No, sir. Bad.

William Aye, well: quite good.

Richard Robert . . .

Robert makes a good putt

Richard Bravo. 'Tis your hit, Mister.
William Aye.
Oxford And you should win with it.)

William misses, quite deliberately, when it would be easier to sink his putt

William No.
Oxford The idea of the game, Mister, is to get your ball down the hole.
William Aye. 'Tis Your Majesty next.

Richard casually and deliberately misses

Richard Missed, dammit. 'Tis your victory Oxford.
Oxford Aye, I'd say so.

Oxford plays the ball behind his back and misses

Oxford Oh gross *merde* of a Turkish donkey! Ah well, a formality, Mayor.
William Is it my hit again? Surely 'tis yours, Majesty!
Richard No.
William I think I just had mine, sire.
Anne You did and then the King did and then Robert did. 'Tis you again.

William mournfully taps the ball into the hole

Richard You won, Mayor.
William I'm sorry, Your Majesty.
Richard Hm. This hole poxes me. Let's make another.
William Another, Majesty?
Richard Aye. A new one.
William Boy, dig another hole.

The servant trowels out another hole

Anne How do you like golf, Mayor?
William Merrily.
Richard You like it merrily? Good. What should I bestow on you now you've won a hole?
William Nothing, Majesty, other than your favour.
Anne Should you be hurt, husband, that the Mayor counts your favour so close to nothing?
Oxford More hurt he refuses a gift from you when he has a-showered you with trinkets.
Richard Aye. I think I sulk somewhat.
William Please sire. Forgive me. I'd delight in a gift.
Richard What would you like then, Mister?
William Um . . .
Richard Name anything.
William I had a case at law, sir. I squabble over houses down Hen Street. I want 'em, my lord, and so do some other bugger.

There is a pause

Richard 'Tis greedy, sir.
William Is it?
Richard What think you, madam?
Anne 'Tis a little greedy.
William Aye, you're right, sire. 'Tis gross.
Oxford True, Mayor . . . not a little greedy: *gross* greedy.
William I'm sorry. I'll drop the suit.
Richard Then let that be my gift: to encourage your generosity.
William Thank you, sire. Thank you. I love this golf. The whole town will
be at golf soon. No pageants soon, for golf games.
Richard Keep the pageant, sir.
William (*quickly*) Right.
Richard I like a play more than anything.
William And I do. And I do. Oh aye. Love a play.
Richard Last year I were at Coventry.
William I heard, sire.
Anne The play there is excellent.
William And here, sire. Excellent.
Richard What does your Guild present? (*He goes to the new hole*) I like not
this hole. Let's have another.
William (*gloomily*) Another.
Richard Aye.
William We could return to the first, sire, and begin again a new round.
Richard No. A new one, eh Robert?
Oxford Oh yes. Definite.
Richard You didn't speak of your pageant, sir.
William (*gloomily*) Oh, 'tis the *Slaughter of the Innocent*, sir.
Richard Ah, the Herod play. Wondrous Herod at Coventry. Very fine. Hair
as red as a furnace.
William Oh, wait till you see ours, sire. 'Tis furious red.
Richard Good. You to start, Mayor.
William Right.

They're putting only from a few yards. William holes out, preferably in one

Anne Oh Mayor! Well hit!
William Oh. A fluke, Majesty. Not intended.
Richard 'Tis the object, Mayor. What did you intend?
William Oh aye, 'tis the object, I know. I intended to be very close with my
first hit. Oh.

At this Alice appears

Alice Majesties. My Lord. Husband. How is the golf?
Anne Your husband plays the game as well as he mayors, madam.
Alice Do he! (*Delighted, to William*) And have you given the King his
winnings?
William Uh.
Richard I win not, madam. In fact, I lose.
Alice Husband, is this true? Do you let a King lose?

William Uh.

Oxford He beats us both, madam. Skilfully.

William As gift for my winning, sire, could I retreat now and count my blessings?

Richard Aye, retreat.

Alice (*furiously*) NO, Mister. You must play again. Do you need a new hole, Majesty?

Richard Aye.

Alice Dig some more holes, Adam. Several.

Anne Your husband was just saying how much he liked the game.

Alice I bet. I mean, 'tis a Royal sport.

Anne Aye.

Alice Aye. I'd like to play myself, me. Do women, madam?

Anne Oh, I expect so.

Alice Then I'll learn.

Anne Splendid. In fact, mistress as your husband has such a talent let him show you. My husband and the Earl will come with me now and I'll pass on the joys of our walk. (*She beams at Richard*) Husband, give the lady your club.

Oxford An' here's mine!

Alice But Majesties!

Anne No buts! 'Tis our pleasure, eh my lords?

Richard Aye. We insist.

William Uh.

Richard What's that, Mayor?

William Nothing, Majesty.

Anne So . . . adieu, mistress. Mayor.

Oxford Aye. Have fun.

Richard, Oxford and Anne exit, gaily

Alice (*furiously*) Ach, William can I ask you a simple question? How is it you have not even the guile to manage to lose a game you cannot play!

William (*heavily*) Boy: stop digging up my green, please, and go away.

The servant exits

Alice (*with club and ball*) *Alors.* I just aims at the hole, do I?

William Madam, my patience is gouged. 'Tis a veritable sieve.

Alice (*concentrating*) Aye? (*She hits the ball well*) Heigh-ho.

William (*very ill*) How many year do I breed this grass, madam?

Alice (*sinking her putt*) There!

William (*exploding*) OH GOD!!

William whacks a ball offstage. There is a glorious smashing of glass

(*Funereally*) Oh, no.

Alice (*looking, and nodding gravely*) 'Tis the Minster glass, William. 'Tis holed in one.

CURTAIN

ACT II

SCENE 1

The Streets

The week of the play. Early morning

Sarah and a befrocked Walter are on their way to rehearsal

Sarah An' will you?

Walter Will I what?

Sarah Play the Christ instead of my Thomas?

Walter I play the fool parading the streets in this frock.

Sarah I may do. I may die. I don't know. Will you play the Virgin? (*Pause*) Walter, I think gold Christs and flows of purple is plays for Italians and not for farthing folk who pack the station at Corpus Christi.

Walter Aye. I know, Sarah. Edward, who is a saint in my mind—which is a simple mind and him but a simple saint—Edward speak of playing the plays with such joy. He hath but few words in it and they gross and cruel but his cheeks ruddy as the pageant draw out next Thursday. 'Tis our man from our guild, as they all be, and all should be.

Sarah Then you'll say no.

They walk

Walter (*uncertainly*) Aye . . . well, I may do.

The Lights open out to encompass the rehearsal space

The rehearsal takes place outside the Pageant House. The wagon is dragged out ready. The players, Will, Edward, Thomas, sit happily on the wagon, as Walter and Sarah approach

Thomas Wife, who is this beauty you've brought?

Will Has a fine rump on her . . . How do, ladies?

Walter How do, Edward?

Edward (*laughing at him a little*) Well, Walter. An' you?

Walter Weary.

Will We'll have no sulking this morning, nips. Edward's missus send us great cake. Thomas is happy. I knows my part backward and the day blesses us.

Walter Then let's start.

Sarah May I watch, gentlemen?

Will Aye. Be our audience. (*To Walter*) And don't tell us you have more changes. Keep that parson out and let's get on with the pageant.

Walter Let's begin then.

Thomas Aye.

Will (*imitating the trumpet fanfare, then announcing proudly*) The Play of the
Pinners, Latterners and Painters: Christ Crucified.

*What follows is a version of the York play No. 35, Crux, Jesus Extensus in ea
super terram. . . . In the rehearsal the play is performed humbly, earnestly and
as beautifully as possible from beginning to end. The performance of Will,
Edward and company is broad, familiar and skilful. The original play is
extraordinary. My version is faithful to its content and style and idiom*

The Passion Play

*The two soldiers enter followed by a bloodied Christ, (Thomas), heaving the
cross*

Soldier One (*played by Will*) This way then nipper. Up on this hill lay down
                the tree
              and strip to striped skin.

Soldier Two (*played by Edward*) I've brought stubs to nail him up
              and mallet to mash them in.

Soldier One   I've brought rope to bind him
              and crown to crown him
              and himself cross to cross him.

Soldier Two   By Christ, he do blaspheme and calls hisself
              many things
              as Saviour, King and God's son.

Soldier One   What say you sir to this event?
              Are you King? And will you rule from this
              tree your kingdom?

Soldier Two   He calls himself nowt now but plays the fool.
              Let's have him up and hear him sing.
              I'll bang the holes in with this tool
              and stretch him out and pull and pull.
              (*He bangs at the cross to make the bore holes*)

Soldier One   Aye, you do that while I crown his head
              and thorn him bloody, thorn him red.
              Till red runs down him, joins the stream
              into a river bed.
              Hail King, Hail Fool, Hail Witch, Hail Pleb!
              (*He crowns Christ, with the crown
              of thorns*)

Soldier Two (*to Christ*) Come bend your back to this tree.

Christ obeys

Soldier One   An' he do, an' he do, quiet as a lamb, see!

Soldier Two   I'll do his hands.

Soldier One   I'll do his feet.

Soldier Two   Cross them and save one nail.

Soldier One   What? Bash it through the two?

Soldier Two   Aye, bash it through the two.
Soldier One   Then that's what I'll do, though 'tis a to-do.
Soldier Two (*having difficulty as he nails Christ to the cross*)
                         Oh shit, that's a pain
                         I've not judged the holes right
Soldier One   Then stretch him again
                         and yank him to that side.
Soldier Two   Done it! by Christ! and broken the bone.
Soldier One   To lug him down here
                         I've broken the toes
                         and smashed all the sinew.
Soldier Two   I'm knackered.
Soldier One   I'm puffed.
Soldier Two   We'll never lift him.
Soldier One   And he can't lift hisself now.
                         That's a sin.
Soldier Two   Well let's go for company to help do this deed.
Soldier One   Aye, that's what we need
                         to mount King onto steed.
Soldier Two   Aye, let's not strain our souls
                         for the sake of this dolt.
                         By Christ, he's a do
                         for four, let alone two.

Soldier One exits, then returns, bringing on two other soldiers, non-speaking

Soldier One   Come on you boys
                         and help heave him high
                         he's off to the tournament
                         between land and sky.
Soldier Two (*investigating*) Have they had his tongue out?
                         He were such a loud mouth.
Soldier One   We'll soon make him sound
                         when we throw him hard down.
Soldier Two   Up boys up.
Soldier One   Heave boys heave!
Soldier Two   By Christ, he's a bugger!
Soldier One   Let's drop him again.
Soldier   See how he do shudder.
Soldier One   That hurt him! That pained!
Soldier Two   Blast! I've done my shoulder.
Soldier One   Shit! I've done my back.
Soldier Two (*kicking the cross*) You sod!
Soldier One   You turd.
Soldier Two   You've got a nerve
Soldier One   Call yourself God!
Soldier Two   Ha! Now he do whimper
                         Were he a real God he'd simper!

Soldier One   Ha! How he do moan.
                         So much for your throne.
Soldier Two   Where is his soldiers come to rescue him?
Soldier One (*spearing Christ's side*) Here's his banner though
                         This red flag on his bones.
Soldier Two (*as they exit*) Come along, boys, let's leave this scene
                         We'll raffle his cloak for a flagon.
                         He's not going to sing, is he
                         Or jump down from our wagon.
                         This so-called King is a worm, not a dragon.
                         And we've threaded him here on the tree
                         So all he'll catch is the sun
                         All he'll catch is his breath
                         All he'll catch is his death and that slowly.

The two soldiers exit

Christ is left alone on the cross, but as he speaks Mary (Walter) enters

Christ   Ah ...
                         Father
                         Forgive them their cruelty.
                         They know nothing of me.
                         They here have me tree'd.
                         For Adam's sin I now bleed
                         and tremble and bleed
                         and pray you will speed
                         to release me from this pain.
                         and I pray

                         Your son swoons dear Lord
                         that all that I suffer may not be in vain
                         but bring down your mercy on men
                         like an endless cleansing rain.
Mary   Alas, my love, my life, my Liege.
                         Alas, mourning now maddens me.
                         Alas, my boy look down on me,
                         Thy mother that did bear thee.
                         You are my fruit, I fostered thee,
                         and gave thee suck upon my knee.
                         Upon my pain have pity.
                         Alas to find my boy above me!
                         Tugged; lugged; broken; tree'd.
                         Nails thrust in and crowned of thorns.
                         To see my birth that I have born bleed
                         tears my heart to tatters ...
                         And though you hang above me wracked on high,
                         I, at the tree's foot, am also crucified.

As soon as the play is finished Thomas jumps down from the cross, laughing

Edward and Will race back on stage, delighted with the play's rehearsal

Only Walter seems gloomy

The Lights cross-fade to the next scene

                    ❧

SCENE 2

The Le Kolves' bedroom. Early morning

Kathryn Le Kolve and Father Henry Melton are in bed. They both wear shifts and take it in turn to delouse each other

Kathryn I must get myself to the Queen.

Father Melton And I to the chapel.

Kathryn The bugs seem to love this cloth particular. (*Meaning his shift*)

Father Melton Is my hair busy?

Kathryn (*exploring and finding a bug*) Here's a plump boy! (*She pops it*) Aye. I will say I like the look of the Earl. He has a fine leg on him.

Father Melton (*producing his leg*) Do I?

Kathryn Very fine but not so influential.

Father Melton Madam, I have access to God ... 'tis more influence than with any King.

Kathryn Aye, but less rare.

Father Melton How less rare?

Kathryn Half the town has the Holy Orders. Only Robert has the King's.

Father Melton True.

Geoffrey (*off*) Madam.

Kathryn Sir.

Geoffrey (*off*) Are you a-bed still?

Kathryn Aye.

Geoffrey (*off*) Is the priest with you?

Kathryn Aye, he ministers to me.

Geoffrey (*off*) Does he?

Kathryn Both to my soul, sir, and to my bugs.

Geoffrey (*off*) Can I come up?

Kathryn (*laughing*) No. (*To Father Melton*) Not when my soul is bared so.

Geoffrey (*off*) What's that?

Kathryn We shall be down by and by, sirrah.

Geoffrey (*off*) We are appointed to attend the Royal Party in the hour.

Kathryn If you are happy to bellow, Mister, we need not dress ourselves but simply stay here and converse with their Majesties so.

Geoffrey (*off*) What, pray, madam, is a husband to do when his wife forbids him entry to the bedroom and then lives her life there?

Kathryn If I could learn you one thing, Mister, it is that nothing was ever solved by whining. 'Tis a dog's solution and not a man's. Spend your wait deciding which of your jewels you will offer to the King and practising your intelligent look.

Geoffrey (*off*) Ach!

Kathryn (*to Father Melton*) I think he quiets. (*She listens*) Yes. 'Tis the whining I can't forgive him for. That and the excessive sweat he make. Unnerve him, Parson, and the liquid dribbles from him. Or excite him, the same. 'Tis hard to clasp a man to you, so slippery.

Father Melton What wear you to the King?

Kathryn Oh, nothing grand, but look . . . (*She gets up from the bed and fishes around in the chest at its foot*) How like you this, Henry? (*It's a handkerchief. She waves it above her head*)

Geoffrey bursts in, clutching a bale of cloth

(*Glowering*) You burst in on us, Mister. I like not to be burst in on.

Geoffrey This has just arrived madam. Think of me as fetcher and carrier. (*He indicates the cloth*)

Kathryn In that case . . .

Father Melton 'Tis the cloak, Kathryn. Marvellous.

Geoffrey Is so much cloth necessary? 'Tis like the Red Sea.

Kathryn Except purple.

Father Melton Are you not stunned by it, sir?

Geoffrey I was stunned more by its cost.

Father Melton Will not be torn, sir. Can be re-used each year. In time 'twill be cheap.

Geoffrey Not in my time.

Kathryn Aye, but husband, will it not now be a most civilized pageant?

Geoffrey 'Twill not be rough. Madam, I find it hard to be delirious of the play when all of us masters in this guild are mortgaged sore to furnish it.

Kathryn Mister, you will bless us for the cost when the King stand by you and gasp at the spectacle.

Geoffrey You're certain he'll come?

Kathryn Sir, the Queen and I will hold hands. She will like my bed best. She will chew my herbs for her curdled womb. I will read to her from my romances. I will not invite her. She will invite herself.

Geoffrey For my part, madam, I understand neither the Queen, nor His Majesty, nor their business with the Earl of Oxford, nor the need of so much cloth.

Kathryn Times change, husband, and needs must change with them.

Geoffrey Aye well, I liked things as they were, when Kings were Kings and a play had less effect and more language.

Kathryn Yes, sir, you has the taste of a labourer!

Geoffrey Aye, I has!

Kathryn Be educated, sir!

Geoffrey Madam, I fork out for your niceties, there is not fat for mine.

Kathryn Ach!

Father Melton A dazzling show and the King would grant you Royal Patent.

Geoffrey You think?

Father Melton I've heard nothing, but I audition many in the confessional and that is the mood.

Geoffrey Hmm.

Kathryn Geoffrey, you are so *pickled*!

Geoffrey An' you would be! My fellows blame me for the cost, my workers set a-mumbling if I enter the shop. My missus calls me oaf, my best apprentice will not swap words at all and I am faulted for being pickled. I am pickled!

Kathryn Husband, we all bear crosses.

Geoffrey Aye, well Walter won't bear his.

Kathryn I have Sarah sullen, and the taxing friendship of a monarch in prospect. Nor am I best well.

Father Melton Please, peace, please! The pageant will be true reward for all our efforts. 'Tis certain our play is a star will outshine all others. I have eyes and ears about the Merchants' rehearsals. They have a vulgar Herod who will say too much, too loud. By contrast we will seem an elegance.

Geoffrey Well, I'm not elegant, me. It would seem more elegance to me were my wife to drape this purple about herself and not the pageant. But I don't know the fashion. I'll get off and leave you to your fashion. Whatever it is.

Geoffrey exits sadly

ı

SCENE 3

The Mayor's house. The bedroom

Anne delouses Richard who delouses Oxford. All are sitting on the bed

Anne Husband, you're crawling.

Richard 'Tis the region, madam. I was clear in London.

Anne Oh sir, that's false: no less than your subjects swarm to feed on you do the fleas come nibbling. You are King to too much life.

Richard Well, I like not being either host to the fleas nor guest of the Mayor.

Anne Would you rather to the Abbey?

Richard God, no.

Oxford Where is the Archbishop?

Richard At war, somewhere. For a man ordained to save souls, he spends much time despatching them to the fires. 'Tis a hard man and a friend now of Gloucester's and Henry Bolingbroke.

Oxford And no friend of mine.

Richard No. He would be Bishop of Westminster and Cardinal. He thinks you barred his way when you were at Court.

Oxford I did. I would have him Bishop of the Channel and swim in his parish.

Anne Robert!

Oxford Well I would. 'Tis a lunatic church, madam, and Christ must
wonder wide-eyed at us. We have two popes and whatever the fashion, to
me they're both a penance: the Frenchman a butcher, the Italian an oaf.
And under their gaze the church is mother to a guild of tinkers and
tonsured criminals for whom heaven hath arrived prematurely on earth.
To call her corrupt is to call water wet and fire hot. His grace the
Archibishop has more land than a Lord *and* more army. He is further
from God than the flea.

Anne (*teasing*) You like him little then?

Oxford (*laughing*) Aye. Little. He and his like marooned me from you both
and would again.

Richard Your head is deserted, Robert. The bugs find little to feast on in
your hair, 'tis too acid there.

Oxford Aye.

Anne Who will search me?

Oxford Us both. Ah, here's a lizard!

Richard And here a toad!

Anne Away! You're toads the pair of you and I'll not tolerate your toady
hands leaping on me.

Richard Toady, toady. (*He tickles Anne*)

Oxford Toady, toady. (*He, too tickles Anne*)

Anne Get off! Anyway, the song of toads is not "toady, toady". So there.

Richard I did not know my Queen was an expert on the toad.

Anne Sir, I married one (*a beat*) and he turned into a prince.

Oxford Bravo.

Richard Madam, you are a joy.

Anne Am I? Then I am a joy with a headache. So let us give audience to
these painters and get us back to bed.

Richard Why are we meeting painters?

Anne Because it suits me!

Richard Oh?

Anne And to keep the waters agitate. A calm surface would show our
Mayor the measure of his folly. This painter is his rival. Let's have them
all in, let's have their beds.

Richard More beds?

Anne The painter's wife begs me to visit hers. I have a letter from her. They
would we watch the pageant from their station.

Oxford She writes? Perhaps *I* should visit her bed.

Anne 'Tis not the pen you would mingle with, Oxford.

Oxford One can mingle with a horse, my Lady, 'tis the conversation one
misses.

Richard Then let us dress ourselves and be kingly for the painter.

Anne I shall go with the mistress, sir. You seduce the man. We'll swap joys
later. Will you give me leave?

Richard Aye Madam.

Richard and Anne kiss

But dally not with your sore head.

Anne Robert.
Oxford Adieu, my Lady.

Anne exits

Sometimes me thinks your Queen is wan, sir, and trembles.
Richard Aye. In the night she grows hot then icy and cries out. The physician bleeds her but does not help, nor quicksilver neither, nor gold. Her health is all my prayer.
Oxford And mine too.
Richard I love her laugh more than the world and will clown all day to hear it. So long as she smiles let's sojourn here.
Oxford And then?
Richard And then back to London and the penitent burghers. 'Tis the season of stubbornness. 'Twill pass as certain as spring follows winter.
Oxford 'Tis not long since you were drowned by this stubbornness.
Richard Was I? Come friend, let's paint this painter a Royal portrait. Is there a crown for me?
Oxford There is, sire.
Richard Then crown me and call in a page or two for the proper effect. Were we in London we could run to a few trumpets and bugger the parliament.

Oxford obliges

The Lights cross-fade to the next scene

SCENE 4

Downstairs in the Mayor's house

Alice enters to find a weary, miserable William

Alice Husband! How is with you?
William Pricked, madam, sorely.
Alice Pricked?
William Aye. Like my grass.
Alice Why so gloomy, Mister?
William Ach! Half my trinkets and best relics dropped on His Majesty without effect. My thorn from Christ's crown: Pfft! Gone. And now His Majesty entertains Le Kolve and his missus by and by. 'Tis forgone between them will lard their way into his pleasure.
Alice I think no, sir. I think we shall outmethod them. I come via the seamstress. I have collected our wipes. And she tells me they have new costumes for the Painters' pageant and a great cloth. I worry not. We has a great Herod.
William (*proudly*) Aye! And we have machines and devices! We have fabulous costumes!
Alice That's it, sir! Worry not on our standing. I'll outgrease Mistress Le

Kolve. I am already confided of headaches and so forth from upstairs.
'Tis a young woman who wants a friend. I'll be it.

Jolyf Absolom enters, dressed in the Herod costume, carrying his mask

Jolyf May I punctuate sir? I come for your feeling re: our rehearsal.
William Come in. Come in, Master Absalom. Your Herod is a marvel, most
monstrous roar and all.
Alice Aye marvellous, and with exploding arse: most devilish!

Jolyf looks proudly at the fireworks attached to the back of his costume

Jolyf So Your Worships is pleased?
William Oh aye. 'Twere a good rehearsal this morning.
Jolyf Aye. 'Twas a ripe showing.
William Show us again.

Jolyf dons his mask

Ha! 'Tis a marvel.

Jolyf roars obligingly and lengthily

Aye, enough now.
Jolyf I am particular pleased with my new phrases.
William Oh?
Jolyf I bring an extra speech or two with me.
William Oh.
Alice Aye, husband, like he refer to York and to our King an' all.
William Oh aye. Aye. Well made.
Jolyf In truth, though I want not coin for it, I've changed a move here and a
move there and a manner. 'Tis better for it.
Alice Well, Mister, my husband did say this morning of your high fee but
evident you earn it.
Jolyf I do, madam. You'd pay as much elsewhere for the voice alone. With
me you get fireworks and new words. 'Tis a complete service.
William Tell me, sir, how compares now our pageant with Coventry?
Jolyf Well, sir, your Herod is superior. And if he is, the pageant is. I'd say
'tis more fearsome than Coventry.
William Is it?
Jolyf Should I share a secret or would you be surprised on the day?
William No, say sir. On the day we has ceremony to stand on and would
not be surprised.
Jolyf We plant our women in the crowd at each station.
Alice Ha!
Jolyf Aye, but here's the rub. Each has in her bundle a pig's bladder loaded
with gore. So when the soldiers come to slaughter the Innocents, each dip
his sword to the bundle like so: in! and splash guts over the crowd and
carry off his bloodied sword aloft.
Alice Oh.
Jolyf Aye, 'tis effective. I anticipate swooning.
Alice So do I, sir.

Kathryn and Geoffrey Le Kolve enter

Kathryn (*briskly*) Felicitations, sir, and how do? Dear sister, a gift! (*She thrusts some flowers into Alice's hand*) Picked from our gardens in Hen Street.

Alice *Merci.*

Kathryn 'Tis a shame your garden is pock-marked so.

Geoffrey How do, Your Worship.

William How do, master. The Queen descends, madam, and will enter shortly. My garden is dug for golf.

Kathryn Golf? (*Anxious not to be out-knowledged*) Oh aye, Golf. (*She pronounces it as if it were French*) Do we intrude, madam? You seem burdened with show business.

William This is Master Absolom.

Geoffrey How do?

William We was just showing him the Herod mask.

Alice And you've been keeping the drapers busy, we hear.

Kathryn Oh . . . (*shrugging*) is your pageant prepared?

William We are so pecked by civic affairs we have small appetite for such luxuries. And yours?

Geoffrey Oh, apparently 'tis fine. How goes our play, Kathryn?

Kathryn Fair, I think. Humble.

Alice Well we was just speaking how much we look forward to viewing it.

Kathryn Then 'tis coincidence mistress. We was just relishing yours.

Anne (*off*) Mistress Selby?

Alice (*simpering*) I am called. (*Shouting*) I come, my Queen. *Excusez-moi.*

Kathryn (*producing a large handkerchief*) *Tout à l'heure.*

Alice (*producing a larger handkerchief*) *Tout à l'heure.*

Kathryn scowls

Jolyf I'll withdraw an' all.

Kathryn Don't mind us, we're just passing. We have royal business you see.

Jolyf No, no, I'll retreat. I'll make an exit.

William Aye, sir, retreat

Jolyf exits

Anne enters

Kathryn prostrates herself. So does Geoffrey. William decides against it then feels at fault and prostrates himself. Anne comes through. Geoffrey has rehearsed his exhortation

Geoffrey Sweet Queen, gracious light of our darkness, lustre of our eye, blush of our cheek, most precious jewel in the crown, receive our humble greetings.

Kathryn Majesty. First woman of our realm and fairest. 'Tis our finest hour to find your favour.

Alice (*gleefully*) 'Tis Geoffrey and Kathryn Kolve, your Royal Highness.

Kathryn (*hissing*) *Le* Kolve.

Alice (*gleefully*) Forgive me, I still think of you as plain Kolve. I forget you have added a Le. Aye, *Le* Kolve, Majesty, of the painters' trade.

Anne To your feet, madam. I cannot curtsey for my head confounds me somewhat. And you, sir. My husband will receive you in the upper storey. I will walk with your wife. (*To Alice*) Mistress Le Kolve has written inviting us to view the pageant from her room. 'Twas a bright note and I will see it.

Kathryn Madam, we are delirious with joy.

Anne I hope not; else us both will wobble on the other to your house.

Kathryn Should I send for a horse, Majesty?

Alice (*smugly*) No, mistress, the Queen likes not to ride.

Anne (*to Alice*) Thank you, Madam Mayor. I should like to ride this once. (*To Kathryn*) Come madam. (*To Geoffrey*) Sir, get you to my husband. (*To William*) Mayor, you could rise, perhaps and lead your friend to the King. *Adieu.*

Kathryn *Adieu* husband. Sir. Madam.

Anne and Kathryn exit

William (*brusquely*) This way, sir.

Geoffrey Thank you, Mister. (*To Alice*) Madam.

Alice (*as the men exit*) 'Tis good the Queen come to your house at this hour. She will see it gets little sun past midday.

Geoffrey True, madam, little glare to distract from the plays.

Geoffrey and William exit

The Lights cross-fade to the Le Kolve house

SCENE 5

Kathryn Le Kolve's bedroom

Kathryn enters with Anne. Anne inspects the bed

Anne 'Tis a marvellous bed, mistress.

Kathryn Aye, Majesty, much cherished.

Anne Has been my choice of gift since I have been to York. I have four.

Kathryn Five, my lady.

The Lights cross-fade to the Pageant House

SCENE 6

Outside the Pageant House

The original cast of the crucifixion play sit brooding on the news of their substitution

Edward And can they undo us so easy?

Will They can do what they will.

Edward 'Tain't really a guild play if none of the guild be in it.

Will Never has been a guild play in that case. We're hardly guild. The masters is the guild not us, and they walks before the wagon or lords it from their window. We're doers in the day for them and doers in the play for them. No more. Took me a bugger to learn them changes.

Edward So you is to be Christ then, Walter?

Walter 'Tis broached but not agreed.

Thomas Aye, well, good luck to you Walter. I'm not grudged. You learned us our parts each year. No need to have done that then, nor feel badly now.

Will No ain't your fault Walter. But I'd say what do pick at the scabs of my anger 'tis we has to find more copper to pay for players to do our play. Makes me spew that do.

Walter Made many of the masters boil an' all, Will. They had to find silver! But the King stir up nonsense in the town. Each gentleman fears disfavour, each outwits himself so as not to be outwitted by others. So 'tis a town on a sudden of no wits, no beds and a thousand wipes.

Sarah 'Tis not the King.

Will Course it is! 'Tis the same Richard who pissed on our dads fifteen year ago. Now he pisses from a greater height that's all. So you can't see his dick but 'tis still dick all right. Ha!

Sarah Fifteen year ago, Will Bluefront, he were a boy and others ruled in his name.

Will 'Tis not what I heard.

Sarah Aye, but you heard last year the Frenchies had landed and that there were a third pope.

Will 'Tis known history, mistress, that the King went back on his word to the commoners.

Walter Aye! In that case 'twill be known history that in thirteen hundred and ninety two the Painters' play were done by new players for the play to be better seen. Is that right?

Will How better seen! Bugger off.

Walter Why then?

Will 'Cause the masters is bloody dense is why.

Edward Walter's right. Say why, Will.

Will Well, we knows why . . . 'tis a fever in the town, 'tis brain pox. (*He can't think, frustrated*) I can't say in one go, why.

Walter An' I'm saying 'tis as likely what happened in the past to the King is as little to do with him being good or bad as us being good or bad now.

Will Not *us*, nipper. *You're* all right.

Walter I'll not do the play without you.

Will Ach!

Sarah (*delighted with Walter*) Oh Walter! And nor I will.

Will Well, you should.

Edward Course you should. Some of us should be up there.

Walter Besides . . . these players from Hull . . . They're rogues who do no

honest labour but simply antic and clown for the big houses. 'Tis a
vagabond lot.

Thomas And I'll certain not have Sarah mingle with them.

Sarah Nor will Sarah have Sarah mingle with them.

Walter Well, there you are. We're out.

Sarah I will not hear the King blamed, sir, nor the Queen. They perceive the
queue of flatterers no less than we do and have been gracious to me in this
stay.

Will I still says is not *our* King any more than, now, is our play.

Edward Course he ain't for us. An' why should he be? The shark is not for
the sprat, Will. No, we is for him. Least I am. And proud of it.

Will Edward, you're proud of every cursed thing. You're proud of that
Minster spire though will kill you and your kin in the making.

Edward Aye, it will. And it will outlive us, just as the King's name will.

Will Ah but *he* won't, Edward. He'll be in the dance of death with the like
of us and Master Le Kolve and the others. We'll all dance and none will
be excused nor substituted.

Edward And what's that got to do with our pageant? I've sulked sufficient,
I'm to bed, me, and meet at Le Kolve's station for the *Corpus Christi*.

Will Oh no! I'm not viewing that play. Sod it!

Thomas Nor me.

Edward Course you will. Come Thursday, you'll be jostling with the rabble
and weeping at the two planks and a passion. And don't say you won't
cause 'tis hollow threat. Nor you, Will.

Will Well I may. I may not.

Edward Well I'll be there from the first and hope for your company. My
missus still bakes her pasties and wish you share them with us.

Will Christ I'd quite forgot that! Can't miss them pasties and all. 'Tis a sore
loss this business.

Walter Aye, I'll be there, Edward, but 'tis no two planks and passion.
'Tis a new fashioned cross and a golden Christ and a purple sea. 'Tis a
spectacle . . . almost wordless.

Will So is our tree abandoned an' all? Ach!

Walter 'Tis all abandoned.

Edward I've half a mind to say let's play it still.

Walter Do what?

Edward No. I just thought.

Thomas I know what you thought, Edward. We could still play our old
pageant and use the old gear and 'twould be no different than ever.

Sarah To what end?

Thomas For our gang.

Will For half the town more like: who'll have no truck for golden Christs.

Walter Aye, but you can't push round the cross illegitimate.

Will More's the point you can't push round the cross with no wagon.

Thomas Then don't push it round. Play it stopped at a station.

Walter Whose?

Thomas Well . . .

Sarah Hen Street! 'Tis not a station but could be.

Thomas Aye. Outside our house, eh love?

Walter And what of the masters? What of mine? Mr Le Kolve will not kiss me for betraying him.

Will 'Tis abandoned gear, we are abandoned players. If a man pick up what is thrown down 'tis no crime.

Walter Aye but we plan to compete.

Will And is competition a crime, then? In which case let the masters dungeon themselves for they will be first to gouge out their own eyes rather than be beaten to it by another. Does not your master undercut mine? Aye, he do, and so we shall play our play more cheaply and bid for the louder hurrah. I'm for it. What of the rest of you?

Thomas Aye, I'm game.

Will Edward?

Edward I s'pose 'tis no great injury. The King will not view it, nor the Mayor nor Mr Le Kolve. 'Twill only be our gang.

Will Then 'tis up to you, Walter.

Walter Must I still speak for the Blessed Virgin?

Will Aye. And I'll scrape your jaw myself.

Walter Then I'll do it, but only for the pasties.

The Lights cross-fade to the next scene

SCENE 7

The Mayor's house. The bedroom

Anne is in bed. Richard, anxious, sleepless, presides over her. She wakes, coughs

Anne Sir, did you sleep well?

Richard Aye, love, and you?

Anne Mmm.

Richard Madam 'tis capital to perjure a King.

Anne I said mmm. Mmm can mean many things.

Richard As: no I did not sleep well but did fever and cry out and tremble so this bed did shudder.

Anne Then you spoke not truly to me, sir. For 'tis not well slept to catch these things.

Richard Mistress. You should be attended by some physician.

Anne I'll have my mother and my own doctor.

Richard They are not here. And they both offend you. Your mother cannot forgive you for your quiet womb and your physic cannot cure you of it.

Anne I chewed on Mrs Le Kolve's herbs for my belly, but 'twere a penance.

Richard I should return you to London.

Anne But will be surrender then, not triumph.

Richard I am confident, sweet, that the maggots there grow shrivelled for want of their apple and will wriggle well enough for his return. We have sent for hint of how the mood prospers. All being well we should return shortly.

Anne 'Tis all being *not* well presses us to.

Richard No, madam, 'tis also true I weary of gaming with these people, and could not make my home here. They come too early to fortune and choke on it.

Anne But if we return, what of Robert?

Richard Madam, rest today, I command it. Tomorrow is the play and a darling day for us.

Anne If I rest what of you, husband?

Richard Oh, Robert and me may ride nearby and bathe or hawk a little.

Anne Or wench a little.

Richard Or wench a little. Aye, you has a stallion's image of me, I would not lose it. And you, do your lovers scale the walls as soon as I depart?

Anne In droves, sir. 'Tis an army. No wonder I tremble.

Oxford (*off*) Majesties?

Richard Robert?

Oxford (*off*) Aye.

Richard Then enter. Do you come to defend my honour against the Queen's paramours?

Oxford Sire, there is news from London.

Richard They want me? See, I said. The vultures still have need of bits to peck at. Well, they must ransom me.

Oxford 'Tis from your uncle. He says the Archbishop returns to York for the *Corpus Christi*.

Richard To what end?

Oxford I know not the motive, my Lord.

Richard Does my uncle ask for my return?

Oxford He speak of the possibility.

Richard The possibility! He speak of the possibility! I am King and there is possibility I return to my own court!

Anne My Lord.

Oxford He reports the Mayor and Sheriffs will welcome you back on certain conditions.

Richard I will not hear of conditions. Conditions is weather and God have control of that and also makes Kings and subjects. Bear back to my uncle, the Regent, that my weather include need of changes, of gales, which will shiver the Mayor and his herd.

Oxford Should I not, instead, report your thanks and gratitude?

Richard No sir! Report as I command.

Oxford 'Tis my experience, sir, that a spit from great distance is no match for a dagger on embracing.

Richard Robert why placate me when 'tis their crew who require your absence from home, and when this chaplain arrives to poison our leisure here?

Oxford No. Not poison. Spice.

Richard How spice?

Oxford Majesty, the Archbishop wants crusades and war against the

French pope. He wants funds for his own knights. He will not kiss our
Mayor here nor his excess on these pageants. Tomorrow will be merry
with bluster from both sides.

Anne Aye. You should join in, sweet, and make fuss of the spectacle, saying
if York be so fat—then should gift more to the nation's purse.

There is a pause

Richard 'Tis two rogues I love.

Anne And who love you.

Richard Aye, report to my uncle our thanks and gratitude. Aye. And let us
tramp outdoor today and leave the Queen to her bedfellows. 'Tis, after
all, a fine day, and if I am still un-Kinged I should enjoy the summer like
any citizen of the realm.

Oxford You will not come with us, Lady?

Anne I grow such a connoisseur of beds, Robert. I must savour them all
day.

Richard The Queen thinks we hunt for maids and not for fish.

Oxford Then let's promise to cook whatever we catch and supper on it.

Anne Best make it young girl then, Robert. Richard says my flesh is tough
now.

Richard Tough? 'Tis unchewable. I'll show you. (*He kisses Anne*) Adieu,
madam, and be waited on.

Anne Aye, sir, and you escape from worry . . . Adieu Robert.

Oxford Adieu Majesty.

Richard I'll send in your woman.

Richard and Oxford exit

Anne alone, coughs violently and pulls the covers over her head

SCENE 8

Downstairs in the Mayor's house

Oxford and Richard prepare for their outing

Oxford So, you'll go back?

Richard Aye, we'll submit. If only to get the Queen to her physic.

Oxford Aye, 'tis reason enough. And I'll go back after tomorrow. I'll take a
horse and ride cross country. Then a boat to Ireland.

Richard I'll go to Ireland in the autumn! We could meet.

Oxford Mmmm.

Richard Except I may be more King then. And chaperoned.

Oxford Well . . .

Richard More King and less Queen. She will not see September but see God
first.

Oxford Come now . . .

Richard No, 'tis fact. She has the most alive mind I know and the least alive body. The one seems to suck out the other too quick.

Oxford She may improve. These things are uncertain.

Richard A new Queen is already arranged for me . . . not yet seven years old. I must be widowed then ringed to a baby. 'Tis a black prospect.

Oxford Then do not remarry.

Richard Oh, Robert, we have an innocent eye of the world. 'Tis a machine and the King is but one cog and no more able to stop its workings than any other. 'Tis a great windmill and will grind us all. I am married to produce . . . to father . . . they give me a new womb to work at, once I have buried my grievance with the city—and buried the woman I love. Then, bereaved of dignity and bereaved of heart, I can stud and be put out to pasture.

Oxford This is bleak, my Lord. We promised to escape from worry. Where would you go?

Richard To the country, sir. To the forest.

Oxford Aye. To forest fires, Richard, and warm, fat, forest haunches. Let's tumble off these humours—let's paddle. Let's baste ourselves.

Richard Oh, sir. I want air, not smothering, not smothering.

Oxford Then let's have air, Majesty. Air all day.

Richard Aye, but fun tomorrow, eh? There is still a little juice left in these York lemons. Let's squeeze out the last drop.

Oxford I never tasted a lemon.

Richard I was sent six from the Roman pope.

Oxford What were they like?

Richard Well, he also sent sugar. Sugar is better.

Oxford Aye, I like sugar.

Richard I have some with me. Shall we taste it?

Oxford Aye.

Richard produces a handkerchief. The sugar is wrapped inside

Richard 'Tis milled fine.

Richard licks his finger and dips it. Then he offers some to Oxford who does the same

The Lights fade to Black-out

SCENE 9

The upstairs window of the Mayor's house looking out onto the street

The idea is that the light on Richard and Oxford in their cups fades to black and this new one flashes up broad Midsummer's Day and noisy and the start of the Corpus Christi *cycle. There are about forty-eight plays in the cycle. The Mayor's play is number nineteen, the Le Kolves', number thirty-five. What happens is that there are twelve stations . . . Le Kolves' perhaps the fourth in order and the Mayor's about eighth. Each play plays all twelve stations; the wagon being pulled from station to station. This all takes a considerable amount of time. It's unlikely that the cycle was completed within the twenty-four hours ... It would be mid-afternoon by the time the Herod play was viewed by anyone and practically midnight by the Crucifixion. The late plays, therefore were lit by torches: an expensive business. Great care would be taken to ensure the plays moved swiftly and efficiently: any traffic jam would have drastic consequences*

The scene starts about seven in the morning at the latest, with the Archbishop, the Mayor and Mayoress up at the window as the Creation Play, play number one, is waiting to start outside. Kathryn and Geoffrey Le Kolve, with Father Melton are also ready at the Le Kolve's window. There would be a huge crowd at each station. The upstairs window above the play is, of course, reserved for the fat cats ... it's the box at the opera. The play is held up for the arrival of King, Queen, and Oxford. This does not please the Archbishop

Archbishop Ach! The plays begin. I think someone really should tell his Majesty that 'tis one thing to miss Holy Mass this morning, 'tis quite another to miss the Creation of the World.

William (*acutely embarrassed and distressed*) 'Tis said he rouses, my Lord.

Archbishop Oh marvellous! The miracle of Genesis and the miracle of his appearance all at once.

Alice We understand the Majesties slept not well.

Archbishop Madam I push in thistles to my mattress to ensure I sleep not well. To sleep heavy is a venial sin, in my opinion.

Alice (*to William*) Should we call down to hold up the start?

Archbishop Aye! Hold up Creation. Good idea. (*Hugely and crassly*) Hold up down there! We wait on the King.

Murmurs are heard from below

Oxford enters blearily

Oxford The King approaches. (*He sees the Archbishop*) Good morning, my lord.

Archbishop Is it the Earl of Oxford?

Oxford Aye.

Archbishop I am amazed, sir. The law exiled you, surely?

Oxford From London.

Archbishop Oh no, sir. 'Twas from the realm.

Oxford The whole realm? Then I should not be here.

Archbishop No sir, you should not.

Oxford 'Tis remarkable. The King and me both thought it were banished from London and the gaze of the new muscle.

Archbishop No, I seen the papers as witness. An' 'tis not new muscle. 'Tis simply muscle long unflexed.

Oxford I'd best be off soon then. To somewhere deeply foreign.

Archbishop Aye, deeply foreign were best, sir.

Oxford How is your hair shirt, my Lord?

Archbishop Installed. (*He pulls at his clothes to reveal it*)

Oxford I hear you wear it even when you take pleasure. That, to me, is the sign of a saintly man.

Archbishop You missed the Mass this morning my Lord. 'Tis a mortal sin.

Oxford Oh I think we'll find a Mass somewhere later on. Surely?

Richard and Anne appear, Anne fragile, Richard hungover

Archbishop Majesty. (*To Anne*) Majesty.

Richard My Lord Archbishop. This is a most pleasant surprise.

Archbishop Ah, if you did not expect me, Majesty, then I am understood why you attended not my Mass and sermon.

Richard No, Lord, we knew of your presence in the town but not of your presence at the Mayor's window. I like not to be told off before the plays and will have Mass later and without preaching.

Richard walks to the window. Applause is heard. He and Anne wave

Richard Do start. An' after God, Mayor, could you manage some breakfast?

God the Father appears, if possible, from a high point in the theatre corresponding to a high point in the street: say an arch of the city walls or a bell tower, to begin the first play, with dazzling light behind him, so as practically to obscure his face (which is a gold mask)

The constant murmur and humour of the crowd dies away to reverence as the character speaks. There is genuine excitement

God   Ego sum alpha and O, vita, via, veritas,
                 Primus et Novissimus.
                 I am gracious and great, God without a
                 beginning; I am maker unmade and all might is in me.

Anne (*clapping her hands*) Oh, I love a good God!

The Lights cross-fade to the Le Kolve house

Later. The Le Kolves' station

Kathryn, Geoffrey, Sarah and Father Melton watch the explosive Herod play; Jolyf is doing his stuff below

Jolyf   No noise nippers. What!
                 Who dares mutter when I appear?
                 Herod—the mighty, marvellous, perfect.
                 Who dares talk
                 when such magnificence come to York!
                 I bluster and blast. I blow and blunder.
                 I crackle and clap and grunt and thunder.
                 I am most terrible, me!
                 Point out a man who is not on his knee
                 and I'll snap off his legs like twigs off a tree.

Kathryn Gross. Ugh!

Father Melton 'Tis a reaction cheaply bought.

Kathryn Do Herod fart? I remember it not from the scripture.

Father Melton The mask is very fine, though, Mister.

Geoffrey Aye, 'tis too fine a mask for the player.

Sarah 'Tis Walter's face Madam. He made it.

Kathryn Did he? Aye, 'tis well done.

Geoffrey Where is Walter! He were bidden aloft.

Sarah Uh. He stays with the others of the old pageant.

Geoffrey Hmm. (*To Kathryn*) What time is the King due?

Kathryn (*watching despite herself*) Sssh!

Geoffrey Sssh not! Beside, the rabble make so much din the play can hardly be heard.

Kathryn Sssh!

Father Melton I think Mister, he is sure to wait until this play is done outside the Mayor's station. That will not be until mid-afternoon before it arrives there even.

Geoffrey Should we wait on our feast, though?

Kathryn (*not looking at him but with half an ear on the conversation*) Husband, we cannot eat before the Royalty arrives.

Geoffrey Madam, our play will not be here until near the midnight. If the King deigns not to enter prior to then, our diet will be too much play, too little food.

Kathryn Oh, he will, he must. Sssh. For heaven's sake.

Geoffrey This King will or must do nothing.

Father Melton Aye. 'Tis true. He attended not the Archbishop's Mass this morning.

Geoffrey We heard he were discovered sleeping with the Queen, Oxford and a horse in his bed.

Kathryn Sssh, please. May not be well done, but 'tis a marvellous story all the same.

The Lights fade on the Le Kolve house and come up on the Selby house

Later, outside the Selby station. Jolyf has reached his patron's station. He elaborates and explodes hugely

Jolyf   Not just Richard come to rest
but three more Kings from East and West arrive with word
of some nipper born in a stable
meant to be saviour, meant to be able to save the world.
No bairn from a barn will compete with me.
I am the biggest and blackest and cruellest and meanest.

Still the Herod play, at the Mayor's window

Richard and Oxford and Anne misbehave. They are at the cold buffet at this most inauspicious time. The Selbys are increasingly desperate to get them to watch

William (*proudly*) This be our pageant, my Lord.

Richard Who's your man?

William He's imported sir.

Richard (*mischievously*) Shame.

William Exceptional red hair on him.

Richard (*mischievously*) 'Tis a wig though, surely.

William (*defeated*) Uh.

Richard (*wandering off*) The man at Coventry had most marvellous hair.

Oxford This one has most marvellous arse!

Archbishop I cannot hear, sir.

Oxford The arse? Why, sir, it explodes noisily.

Archbishop The play!

Richard Who's hungry?

William My Lord, we thought to eat *after* the play!

Archbishop 'Tis very broad this show and foul.

William Uh.

Archbishop 'Tis not meet to inflate Herod so.

Oxford Why's that, my Lord?

Archbishop These pageants give too much air to evil and insufficient to good.

Alice Well, surely Lord, the evil parts is best fun.

Archbishop Madam, 'tis the feast of Christ's Body, not a funfair.

William and Alice are upset that nobody watches the play during this dispute

Oxford Aye, Reverend, but a pageant of Christ and Mary and Angels would send the rabble asleep.

Archbishop That's blasphemy, sir.

Oxford (*enjoying himself hugely*) No, 'tis fact. A fact cannot be blasphemy, can it?

William Please sir, you miss the play!

Richard I know. (*To Alice*) 'Tis your cooking, madam. 'Tis a temptation. Robert, you should taste this chicken!

Alice (*hysterically*) No! Please! Watch the play! Please!

Archbishop In my opinion, these plays grow annually more vulgar. 'Tis a procession of guts and violence and lewd laughter. 'Twere the subject of my message this morning.

Richard And we missed it.

Alice (*frustrated*) Sirs, he made reference to the King.

Richard Who?

Alice The Herod.

Richard The Herod? What reference?

Alice He mentioned Your Majesty and the town.

Richard Did he? And we missed that an' all. Can he repeat it?

Alice Uh.

Anne Why?

Alice Why? Madam?

Anne Aye, why?

Alice Why what?

Anne Why did the Herod mention my husband?

Alice Uh ... (*To William*) Why, husband?

William Out of topicality.
Richard Oh, topicality! Did he mention my Lord the Archbishop?
William Uh. I don't recall.
Richard (*impishly*) You're not mentioned, my Lord. Not topical enough.
Archbishop I cannot follow this play for the buzz up here.
Oxford Buzz? Who buzzes? Do you buzz my lady?
Archbishop The din you make, my Lords!
Oxford ⎫
Richard ⎬ (*together*)   Oh, the din, the din!
Anne ⎭
William My Lords, please! 'Tis the killing of the babes to come.

Below, Jolyf continues

Jolyf   I am the biggest and blackest and cruellest and meanest.
           I've sent out soldiers to scour the town
           and butcher all brats to bits and pieces. Tomorrow I'll
           breakfast on babby bacon and childy chops and smoked nipper
           and infant pie and guarantee that come tonight there'll be no
           tiny Messiah. There'll be no star in the sky.
           There'll only be me, horrible Herod,
           There'll only be myself, there'll only be I!

*Herod's soldiers splash the guts of the butchered babies. The Archbishop is
flecked*

Archbishop By Christ! I am all a-bloodied.   .
Oxford You are, my Lord. Your ermine looks freshly killed.
Archbishop Ach!
Alice I sicken sir.
William (*in despair*) Oh, madam!
Anne Oh dear!
William Oh God. Don't swoon, please.
Anne I think she do, Mister.

Alice faints

Oxford Aye. There she goes.
Archbishop Is there mess on my face?
Oxford Um. (*He inspects gravely*) 'Tis hard to say, Lord.
Archbishop I must go in and clean myself. Ach!
William (*abjectly*) My Lord, you'll miss the play.
Archbishop Would it had missed me, sir!

   The Archbishop exits, flicking imaginary blood from his clothes

The Lights cross-fade to the Le Kolve house

Minutes to midnight, back at the impatient Le Kolves'

Geoffrey (*funereally*) 'Tis our play next madam.
Kathryn Some minutes off.

Geoffrey Some minutes! The day is finished and no King. How much later can he be and not miss it?

Kathryn Some minutes. Sarah has fetched them. Calm yourself.

Geoffrey Do you know the bill of the play?

Kathryn Aye, you said.

Geoffrey God's teeth. And I starve madam!

Kathryn You had food earlier.

Geoffrey 'Twould not fill a rabbit.

Kathryn Sir, more will spoil your feast. Shut up now. You'll thank me for it later.

Geoffrey You said that earlier.

Kathryn Aye, I said earlier you'd thank me later and so you will.

Father Melton Sir, we are in good stead. Each pageant processes, none to rival ours. 'Tis a triumph. Our crowd is vast and high spirited and will hurrah us.

Geoffrey (*in a voice of doom, looking out and down the street*) See! 'Tis our pageant.

Kathryn Is it?

Geoffrey Aye, madam. It comes.

Kathryn Bother.

Geoffrey *It* comes but the King comes not. 'Tis wasted. (*He sits down*) Ach! (*Murmuring*) Blessed Virgin Mary, Mother of God. 'Tis complete wasted. 'Tis money melted. 'Tis harvest rotted. 'Tis feast unfeasted. I said this would happen. God, God, God.

Kathryn I bet 'tis the Mayor. I see his hand in this, or his shrew. They sulk so miserable after their flat affair they cannot bear the King to see ours. Witch!

Father Melton Can we not send horses?

Geoffrey We can send nothing with the wagons cramming the roads.

Kathryn Then we'll wait.

Geoffrey Can't.

Kathryn We can. We says "Wait!" and they wait.

Geoffrey 'Tis an offence and will be fined: six shillings and eight pence.

Kathryn Then we will be fined but the King will see the play.

Geoffrey The additional torches?

Kathryn Sir, we are in danger of losing everything and you carp at torches!

Geoffrey Do you know the price of a torch, madam?

Kathryn Please don't tell me.

Geoffrey We paid Margaret Chandler fourteen shillings for six.

Kathryn Will you cry wait to them?

Geoffrey Ach.

Kathryn Then *I* will, and I'll barge through the throng also to fetch this King. Since no-one else offer. If you want something doing, Kathryn, do it yourself.

Kathryn stomps off

SCENE 10

The Streets

The Royal party walk with Sarah to the Le Kolves' house. It is dark and in the distance light and noise come from the various stations

Sarah Sir we must hurry.
Richard Must we?
Sarah Aye. That were the pageant before the Cross play we passed.
Anne Aye, Richard, let's be swift. 'Tis my favourite and has Sarah's husband in it. He do the Christ.
Sarah No, he don't madam. They've changed the crew.
Anne Oh?
Sarah Aye. To flatter you. They have foreign players. They have a maid to play the Mary.
Oxford A woman?
Sarah Aye. They wanted me.
Oxford Well, that's novel. Is she pretty?
Sarah She come from Hull!
Oxford Aye, but do she come prettily from Hull?
Anne Sir, hold up a second. (*She coughs and holds her side*)
Richard Madam?

Anne coughs violently

Anne God. (*She sinks down to the ground*)
Oxford Majesty, do you sicken?
Anne Aye. (*She coughs into her handkerchief. It comes away from her mouth bloodied*)
Sarah Oh ma'am, you bleed!
Anne Aye, it seem so.
Sarah My Lord. There is my house nearby. 'Tis poor but you are welcome to rest up there awhile. And . . . you could watch the old Cross play . . . if you wished to. My husband's boys play it there for their own gang.
Anne I'd like that. Richard.
Richard Let's to it. We'll carry you, darling.
Anne Aye and get me to a bed, sir.
Richard (*worried*) Madam you are a devil for a bed.
Sarah This way, my Lord.

They struggle off

The Lights cross-fade to the Le Kolve house

SCENE 11

The Le Kolves' house

The position of the house has changed so that now we see less front on and therefore beyond the house catch a glimpse of the new wagon complete, in the flickering torchlight, with all-gold Christ. Acres of purple and some soldiers hanging around waiting to begin. There are restless sounds from the unseen crowd

Geoffrey is suicidal at the window. There is a noise below

William and the Archbishop enter angrily

William Mister, what is the meaning of this delay? The wagons jam up behind.

Geoffrey We wait on the King, sir.

William The King? The King left my house an hour ago to join you.

Geoffrey He come not.

Archbishop This King needs no fool to entertain him. He do the job for himself. 'Tis an outrage.

William By Christ, our day is poxed by his manners and we are the laughing stock, sir. He yapped, him and his two dogs, through our pageant and now will dodge yours altogether.

Archbishop Aye, Mister.

William No more. Go ahead, sir.

Geoffrey (*adamant*) I'll not. The King must view the play.

William The King, Mister, may be in Coventry for all we know.

Geoffrey Sir, has broken us, the brunt of this pageant and the King *must* view it. There's a gold Christ and a purple sea.

Archbishop A gold Christ. 'Tis inappropriate. 'Tis pagan.

Father Melton Oh no, my Lord, 'tis majestic.

Archbishop 'Tis unchristian, Parson. We'll have sacrifices next.

William We'll have the play next and now. Or I'll call in the sergeants.

Kathryn and Alice enter

Kathryn Husband, order the play started.

Geoffrey Do the King appear?

Kathryn He does not, sir, but our old pageant starts up outside a private station.

Geoffrey What's that?

Kathryn The men from the play, your apprentice and gang, make the old pageant. Now our play play not, the crowd wander down to view it. Soon will be deserted below.

Alice 'Tis a devil, this business, and I sorrow for you, mistress.

Kathryn Thank you, my Lady.

Alice Our day is spoiled an' all. And I've swooned.

Kathryn Dear madam, friend Mayor, my Lord, let's view the pageant severally. King or no King.

Alice Thank you madam.

William My Lord, the Archbishop, tells us this is the colour of his Majesty. Unworthy of the crown. Our brothers in London know it and work on it.

Geoffrey Do they? (*To Kathryn*) I smelled that from the off.

William Aye and we should learn, eh, Archbishop?

Archbishop You should.
William So sit eh? And be peaceful.
Archbishop Is there blood in this pageant?
Father Melton None, my Lord. 'Tis a serene cross.
Archbishop Well that's something.
Kathryn Do we start then husband?
Geoffrey Aye, we start. Go to, down there, and begin.

The crowd roar their approval. Trumpets sound. The burghers, together,
united, hold their handkerchiefs aloft, waving them like banners

SCENE 12

Hen Street. A hut

Anne is in Sarah's bed. Richard sits by her. Sarah and Oxford stand facing
front half-watching the play: the old Cross play. In the background throughout
the new Pageant proceeds, illuminated from time to time by a torch which
shows the golden Christ crucified, then later the ubiquitous purple sea

Anne I am feeble, sir.
Richard You're drained, sweet, 'tis too long a day and too much sport.
Anne Aye.
Richard How's the bed?
Anne Oh. Fine.
Richard Best bed?
Anne Most welcome, sir.
Richard Then sleep, eh love?
Anne (*regretfully*) I miss the passion play.
Richard Aye. 'Tis a rough and ready one proceed outside.
Anne Can I not view it?
Richard Madam, you can sleep.
Anne I can sleep later. Can I not be pushed to the window?
Richard Robert?
Oxford Aye, my Lord?
Richard How is the play?
Oxford Humble, sir. Very special.
Richard Then help me drag the Queen's bed to the doorway.
Oxford Aye, most willingly.

Richard and Oxford drag the bed down to the doorway

Richard Can you see, my lady?
Anne Almost.
Richard (*helping Anne, gently*) Let's plump up more cushion. There.
Anne Aye! I can see now: oh, the Christ have a fine leg on him.
Oxford Aye, he do.
Sarah 'Tis my husband, madam.
Anne (*smiling weakly*) Is it, Sarah? I like a nice Christ.

Richard Madam, this is the most dilute apology to spend your life in bed.
Anne Shut up, Richard.
Richard Must I take you back to London still in it?
Anne Aye. Come you both, sit by me, 'tis a fine view.

They watch. A long pause. We can hear some of the text from the play. At length Oxford looks to Anne for her response. She's rapt

Oxford You're weeping, madam.
Anne I do, Robert. I always forget, 'tis such a cruel play.

CURTAIN

FURNITURE AND PROPERTY LIST

The striking of furniture etc. is not indicated as some furniture can remain set, and much will depend on the nature of the production.

ACT I

SCENE 1

Off stage: Two planks **(Will and Edward)**
Rope **(Will or Edward)**
Tray piled with breadcakes, a jug of beer and pots **(Sarah)**

SCENE 2

On stage: Bed with canopy, table and chair

Personal: **Richard:** handkerchiefs (at least six)

SCENE 4

On stage: Bed with canopy, table and chair

SCENE 5

On stage: Table laden with food, chairs

SCENE 6

Personal: **Alice:** orange, stuck with cloves etc.

SCENE 7

On stage: Tools to suggest workshop
Screen

SCENE 8

On stage: (*if possible*) Lawn

Off stage: Golf gear, club and ball **(Richard, Oxford and William)**
Trowel **(Servant)**

ACT II

SCENE 1

On stage: Wagon

Off stage: Cross. Nails, mallet, rope and crown of thorns for Passion Play **(Will, Edward and Thomas)**

SCENE 2

On stage: Bed
Chest. *In it:* handkerchief

Off stage: Bale of cloth **(Geoffrey)**

SCENE 3

On stage: Bed with canopy, table and chair

SCENE 4

Off stage: Mask **(Jolyf)**
Flowers **(Kathryn)**

Personal: **Jolyf:** Fireworks on costume
Kathryn: Handkerchief
Alice: Handkerchief

SCENE 5

On stage: Bed
Chest

SCENE 7

On stage: Bed with canopy, table and chair

SCENE 8

Personal: **Richard:** Handkerchief with sugar wrapped inside

SCENE 9

On stage: *In Selby area:* table with cold buffet, chairs
In Le Kolve area: chairs

Personal: **Soldiers:** Blood, etc., to spread around

SCENE 10

Personal: **Anne:** Handkerchief

SCENE 11

On stage: Decorated wagon

Personal: **Burghers:** Handkerchiefs

SCENE 12

On stage: Bed with cushions
Chair
Wagon and rest of pageant, the Cross and purple material

LIGHTING PLOT

ACT I

SCENE 1

To open: General exterior lighting, late May, early morning

Cue 1   Kathryn exits   (Page 11)
Cross-fade to next scene

SCENE 2

To open: Low interior lighting in acting area, but bright outside shuttered window

Cue 2   **Anne:** "Away with them!"   (Page 14)
Cross-fade to next scene

SCENE 3

To open: Interior lighting

Cue 3   **Alice:** "I know. Let's go up, eh?"   (Page 16)
Cross-fade to next scene

SCENE 4

To open: Low interior lighting (as in Scene 2)

Cue 4   From inside the closed canopy, giggles   (Page 18)
Cross-fade to Le Kolve area

SCENE 5

To open: General interior lighting

Cue 5   Kathryn runs off   (Page 21)
Cross-fade to street area

SCENE 6

To open: Bright exterior lighting

Cue 6   Alice and Sarah exit   (Page 23)
Cross-fade to next scene

SCENE 7

To open: Low interior lighting

Cue 7   Geoffrey and Father Melton exit   (Page 26)
Cross-fade to next scene

SCENE 8

To open: Bright exterior lighting

Cue 8 **Alice:** "'Tis holed in one."   (Page 30)
          Fade to Black-out

ACT II
SCENE 1

To open: Exterior, early morning light, covering part of stage

Cue 9 **Walter:** "Aye ... well, I may do."   (Page 31)
          Open out exterior light as the action moves

Cue 10 Edward and Will race on   (Page 35)
          Cross-fade to Le Kolve area

SCENE 2

To open: Interior lighting

Cue 11 Geoffrey exits   (Page 37)
          Cross-fade to Selby area

SCENE 3

To open: Low interior lighting

Cue 12 **Richard:** "and bugger the parliament."   (Page 39)
          Cross-fade to next scene

SCENE 4

To open: Interior lighting

Cue 13 Geoffrey and William exit   (Page 42)
          Cross-fade to Le Kolve area

SCENE 5

To open: Interior lighting

Cue 14 **Kathryn:** "Five, my lady."   (Page 42)
          Cross-fade to next scene

SCENE 6

To open: General exterior lighting

Cue 15 **Walter:** "Then I'll do it, but only for the pasties." (Page 45)
          Cross-fade to Selby area

SCENE 7

To open: Fairly low interior lighting

Cue 16 Anne pulls the covers over her head   (Page 47)
          Cross-fade to next scene

Scene 8

To open: Interior lighting picks out Richard and Oxford

Cue 17   Oxford and Richard both lick sugar   (Page 48)
            Fade to Black-out

Scene 9

To open: Black-out

Cue 18   When ready   (Page 49)
            *Bright exterior lighting in main area, less bright interior lighting
            in Selby area*

Cue 19   God the Father appears   (Page 50)
            Bring up dazzling light behind him

Cue 20   **Anne:** "Oh, I love a good God!"   (Page 50)
            *Fade light behind God the Father and cross-fade lights from Selby
            area to Le Kolve area*

Cue 21   **Kathryn:** "... but 'tis a marvellous story all the same."   (Page 51)
            Fade lights on Le Kolve area and bring up on Selby area

Cue 22   **Jolyf:** "I am the biggest and blackest and cruellest and mea-
            nest."   (Page 51)
            Fireworks, then bring up lights in Selby area

Cue 23   The Archbishop exits   (Page 53)
            Cross-fade to Le Kolve area

Cue 24   Kathryn exits   (Page 54)
            Cross-fade to external area

Scene 10

To open: Night time, occasional distant glimmer of torchlight from the
            pageant

Cue 25   All exit   (Page 55)
            Cross-fade to Le Kolve area

Scene 11

To open: Dim, interior lighting in Le Kolve area, maintain flickering
            torchlight in external area

Cue 26   The crowd roars. Trumpets sound   (Page 57)
            Cross-fade to next scene

Scene 12

To open: Dim interior lighting, maintain flickering, occasional torchlight
            in background

Cue 27   **Anne:** "I always forget 'tis such a cruel play."   (Page 58)
            Fade to Black-out

EFFECTS PLOT

ACT I

Cue 1   When ready   (Page 1)
Bells sound to indicate five o'clock

Cue 2   **Father Melton:** "Aye, do the moves."   (Page 9)
Loud and extended ringing of bells

Cue 3   **Geoffrey:** "The King comes!"   (Page 9)
The bells stop ringing

Cue 4   William whacks a golf ball offstage   (Page 30)
Sound of glass smashing

ACT II

Cue 5   When ready at beginning of Scene 9:   (Page 48)
Background noise of crowd

Cue 6   **Archbishop:** "... We wait on the King."   (Page 49)
Crowd murmurs

Cue 7   Richard walks to the window   (Page 50)
Applause

Cue 8   God the Father appears   (Page 50)
Murmur from crowd dies

Cue 9   **Jolyf:** "I am the biggest and blackest and cruellest and meanest."   (Page 51)
His fireworks explode

Cue 10   As the Royal Party walk to Le Kolve's house   (Page 55)
Background noise of pageant

Cue 11   When ready at the beginning of Scene 10   (Page 55)
Restless noises from crowd

Cue 12   **Geoffrey:** "... Go to, down there, and begin."   (Page 57)
The crowd roars. Trumpets sound

Cue 13   **Anne:** "Aye. Come you both, sit by me, 'tis a fine view."   (Page 58)
Some of the text of the Passion play is heard

MADE AND PRINTED IN GREAT BRITAIN BY
LATIMER TREND & COMPANY LTD, PLYMOUTH
MADE IN ENGLAND